A JAPANESE TOUCH FOR YOUR HOME

A JAPANESE TOUCH

Photographs by **Ryo Hata**

FOR YOUR HOME

Koji Yagi

HOME

KODANSHA INTERNATIONAL
Tokyo • New York • London

The publisher would like to thank the following for their assistance:

Barbara Curtis Adachi, Daitoku-ji (Koho-an), Hasshokan Restaurant, Kakusho Restaurant, Kenchiku Shicho Kenkyujo, Kitcho Restaurant, Matsuishi Tatami, Nishi Hongan-ji, Takumi Ohsawa, Sakai City Museum, Kiyoshi Seike, Shibundō, Shinkiraku Restaurant, Hajime Shimokawa, Shokokusha Publishers, Shou-en, Miwa Takano, Yoshihiro Takishita, Urasenke Foundation, Wafu Kenchikusha Publishers, Shinichi Yamamoto, and Tadao Yoshijima.

Photo Credits:

Yukio Futagawa, p. 71 (bottom); Japan Travel Bureau, p. 6 (bottom); Susumu Koshimizu, p. 5 (center), p. 8 (bottom), Pls. 8, 11, 17, 19, 25, 27, 28, 35, 44, 45, 56, 57, 58, 62, 64, 66, 68, 85, 86, 87, 88, 91, 94, 98, 102, 108, 109, 110, 111, 117, back jacket (top right, top left); Tadahiro Kumagai, Pl. 119; Hiroaki Misawa, p. 71 (top left); Kazuyoshi Miyamoto, p. 71 (center); Toru Nakagawa, p. 70 (bottom); Haruzo Ohashi, p. 19 (top); Tsuneo Sato, p. 71 (top right); Eitaro Torihata, p. 58 (bottom); Tohru Waki (Shokokusha), p. 67 (center right, center left, bottom).

Illustration Credits:

P. 8 (Hickox House): Redrawn from *The American House* by Mary Mix Foley © 1979, Harper & Row, and reprinted by permission of the publisher. This material is after a photograph by Henry Fuermann, as published in *Frank Lloyd Wright to 1910* by Grant Carpenter Manson. Copyright © by Van Nostrand Reinhold Company. Reprinted by permission of Van Nostrand Reinhold Company. P. 8 (Gamble House): Redrawn from *The American House* by Mary Mix Foley © 1979, Harper & Row, and reprinted by permission of the publisher. This material is after a photograph by Maynard L. Parker, collection of James Marston Fitch, and reprinted by permission of the owner.

Architects/designers of the houses illustrated:

Araragi Architects, Pls. 26, 75; Toshinori Fukaya, Pl. 52; Masao Hayakawa, p. 71 (top right); Shigezo Hirai, Pls. 44, 98; Hirata Construction Co., Pls. 11, 16, 27, 58, 87, 99, 111, 113, back jacket (top left), p. 5 (center), p. 59 (center), p. 63 (top, bottom); Masayuki Imai, Pls. 19, 25, 109; Akira Irinouchi, Pl. 57; Hiroyuki Ishida, Pls. 51, 67; Ishima Construction Co., Pls. 24, 93, 97, 112, p. 63 (center right); I.S.S. Associated Architects and Engineers, Pl. 104; Satohiro Kawai, Pls. 15, 101; Noriyoshi Kawazoe, Pls. 28, 35, 108, 117; Kikuchi Construction, back jacket (bottom right); Kindai Architectural Consultants, Pl. 89; Kazuyoshi Komachi, Pls. 83, 94, 110; Komagura Architects, Pls. 21, 37, 56, 77, 84, 106; Tsugio Kosukegawa, Pls. 9, 13; Toshimasa Kozaki, Pl. 62; Toshiro Kubodera, Pls. 45, 64, 68, 91; Takashi Kurosawa, Pl. 42; Shosuke Maki, Pls. 55, 60; Masuzawa Architects and Associates, p. 59 (top); Togo Murano, p. 71 (top left, center); Hitoshi Nagao, Pl. 90; Shosei Nakamura, Pls. 5, 63, 92, 95, back jacket (bottom center); Motoi Nanasawa, Pl. 86; Fumio Ogishi, Pl. 8; Harutaka Ohishi, Pl. 4; Okuno Construction Co., Pl. 100; S. Takagi and Associates, Pl. 121; Asohiko Sakamoto, p. 59 (bottom); Kozo Sano, Pls. 14, 31; Shinahara Architects, Pl. 73; Naoharu Shishiuchi, Pl. 65; Yoshio Shoya, Pl. 71; Sohara Kikuchi and Associates, Pls. 17, 66; Ikuo Suzaki, Pls. 29, 78; Ryoji Suzuki, Pl. 6; Hidezo Takada, p. 58 (bottom); Susumu Takasuga, Pls. 3, 54, 61, 76, 102, 105, front jacket, title page; Seisaku Taniguchi, Pls. 7, 22, 43; Takashi Taniyama, Pls. 1, 103, p. 5 (bottom); Katsushi Tatamiya, Pls. 20, 70; Sadao Tsuneoka, p. 107; Atsushi Uchida, Pl. 53; Ueno Construction Co., Pl. 41; VA · COM, Pls. 18, 50; Fujio Yamamoto, p. 58 (top); Yasui Moku Construction, Pls. 85, 88, back jacket (top right); Isoya Yoshida, p. 70 (bottom); Junzo Yoshimura, Pls. 2 (garden designed by Harunaga Yanoguchi), 10, 72, 120 (garden designed by Harunaga Yanoguchi), p. 67 (center right, center left, bottom).

Line drawings by Kinji Kuwata.

THE AUTHOR

Koji Yagi was born in 1944 in Aichi Prefecture, Japan, and graduated from the Department of Architecture of the Tokyo Institute of Technology in 1969. From 1971 to 1974, he worked with the Syrian government as a technical advisor sent by the Overseas Technical Cooperation Agency of Japan. From 1975 to 1976, he was with the Tropical Building Research Group at Queensland University in Australia, conducting research on indigenous housing of the South Pacific. In 1980 he was a visiting assistant professor at the University of Oklahoma, affiliated with the Environmental Design Department. Mr. Yagi currently teaches and does research at the Tokyo Institute of Technology. In addition, he is a practing architect. He recently translated into Japanese *The American House* by Mary Mix Foley, and contributes regularly to leading architectural journals in Japan.

THE PHOTOGRAPHER

Ryo Hata was born in 1943 in Ishikawa Prefecture, Japan, and graduated from the Department of Art of Nihon University. A free-lance photograher who has published in numerous Japanese magazines, Mr. Hata specializes in Japanese gardens and houses.

Distributed in the United States by Kodansha America, Inc., 114 Fifth Avenue, New York, N.Y. 10011, and in the United Kingdom and continental Europe by Kodansha Europe Ltd., 95 Aldwych, London WC2B 4JF. Published by Kodansha International Ltd., 17-14 Otowa 1-chome, Bunkyo-ku, Tokyo 112, and Kodansha America, Inc. Copyright © 1982 by Kodansha International Ltd. All rights reserved. Printed in Japan.

LCC 82-80646
ISBN 4-7700-1662-X

First edition, 1982
First paperback edition, 1992
95 96 10 9 8 7 6 5

CONTENTS

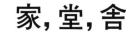

家,堂,舍

House   Entrance

House and Other Buildings

INTRODUCTION

Building Construction

If we look at ancient Egyptian hieroglyphs used to depict a house and entrance, we will see that the hieroglyphs focus upon the walls. Perhaps this reflects the way in which buildings were constructed there—by building up from the foundation. This emphasis on walls, which was to influence the evolution of Western architecture, presumably developed from the need to provide a comfortable interior sheltered from the harsh climate.

If we look at the Japanese writing system, based on characters borrowed from the Chinese, we will see that the characters for house and other buildings all contain the topmost element, the roof. This reflects the Japanese process of housing construction—erecting a wood outer frame and covering it with a roof before making the inner walls. This emphasis on the roof may have developed as a result of the requirement that houses offer shelter from the rain while permitting cross ventilation in the hot and humid summer of Japan. In this way we can find a major conceptual difference between Western and Japanese attitudes toward architecture.

In Japanese house construction, a wood frame is built first, followed by the raising of the roof, and then the addition of walls.

The physical division of space in a timber-framed Japanese house characteristically occurs after the roof is raised, unlike the traditional Western method of building in stone, where the walls separating each room are built first and the roof put in place afterward, creating in the end a whole of separate spatial units. The interface between interior and exterior is also different. In masonry construction, a solid wall separates inside and out and is structurally important, so that few openings are permitted. Wood frame construction in Japan, on the other hand, requires no enclosure between the supporting posts and, with the use of movable partitions, it is possible at any time to open interior and exterior spaces to each other. This style of wood construction allows a step-like hierarchy of spaces. Again, with the thick walls of masonry construction, one room is much like another as far as separation goes, but with paper-covered sliding doors, the degree of separation increases with the number of partitioning agents. In the deepest part of the Japanese house, that is, the middle, is the plastered wall, along which are arranged the sleeping rooms. Beyond these are more open and functionally free spaces, divided into any number of rooms by sliding doors, and surrounding these is a wide corridor bounded at the outside by wooden shutters which offer protection from the rain and cold. The eaves extend well beyond these doors, creating a buffer space appropriate to Japan's rainy climate.

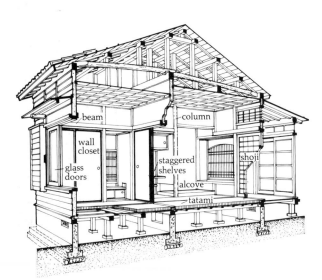

Section of a Japanese house.

Climate

Japanese architecture, like any other architecture, is deeply influenced by the environment. In addition to the four seasons, there are a short rainy season in early summer and typhoons in early fall, creating a cycle of six "seasons." Spring and autumn are pleasant, and winter, of course, is cold. The three remaining seasons—the rainy season, summer, and typhoon season—are hot and muggy, and it is to these three that Japanese architecture is geared. The assumption is that if a house is constructed to ameliorate the discomfort of rain and humidity, the human

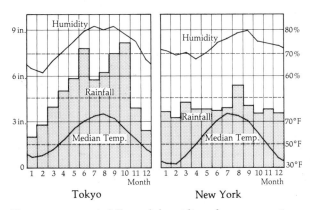

Temperature, rainfall, and humidity chart comparing Tokyo and New York.

6

body can bear the discomfort of the only remaining season that poses a problem, winter.

A Culture of Wood and Paper

To cope with the warm and humid climate of Japan, materials with a low thermal capacity, such as wood, are best, and to cope with the frequency of earthquakes, materials such as brick or stone are avoided. Fortunately, Japan is blessed with good raw materials, particularly timber, well suited to the climate and ideal for an earthquake-prone country. The abundance and variety of wood has, as a result, instilled in the Japanese a keen appreciation of wood—its luster, fragrance, and texture.

As will be seen in this book, wood, paper, and other native materials are copiously used in the home. The shoji sliding doors made of soft, translucent paper and delicate wood latticework, the heavier *fusuma* sliding doors covered with paper of subtle or bold designs, the bamboo and reed screens, the handsome wood pillar in the alcove, the lovely paper lampshades with wood bases, and, of course, the bath made of aromatic cedar all attest to the Japanese love of wood and paper.

Asymmetry

The Japanese concept of beauty incorporates none of the symmetry that is to be found in pre-modern Western and traditional Chinese perceptions of beauty. In symmetry, left and right, size, and volume are orchestrated to create perspective and balance. In asymmetry, the balance between left and right is altered to create a dynamic beauty.

Japanese flower arrangement (*ikebana*) enthusiasts will probably recall their first encounter with this art form with amusement, for the temptation must have been to construct a neat arrangement of equal numbers of flowers contained within a perfectly round or square perimeter. Though, of course, circles and squares do exist in Japanese design, it is the triangle that defines Japanese flower arrangement, and three main stems—long, medium, and short—are arranged in a triangular area in exciting, but comfortable, tension.

In terms of architecture, Buddhist temples built under strong Chinese influence in Japan in the eighth century had already begun to alter the imported aesthetic of symmetry by allotting different emphasis to different parts. A fine example is the Horyu Temple compound in Nara in western Japan where two unequal masses, the tall, slender pagoda and the low, wide Golden Hall, stand alongside each other. Here, again, one can see the aesthetic of dynamic tension asserting itself.

It is difficult to explain the Japanese love for asymmetry, yet it cannot be unconnected with their perception of nature. If, as proposed by a Japanese anthropologist, Western culture originated in the world of the desert, then perhaps the desert dwellers' view of the universe gave birth to monotheism and saw beauty in perfect symmetry that has little relevance to nature as a whole. And, if, in contrast, Japanese culture is seen to have originated in the chaotic world of the forest, then perhaps the pantheism that evolved led to an appreciation of the unbalanced harmony in the tension created by dynamic forces locked in unresolved conflict.

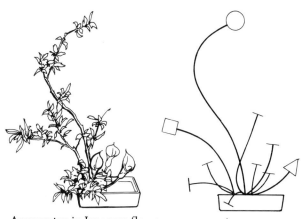

Asymmetry in Japanese flower arrangement.

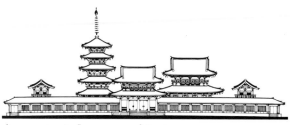

Asymmetry in Japanese architecture.

The texture of wood is an important part of Japanese aesthetics.

Cedar forest in the northern hills of Kyoto.

Warren Hickox House, Illinois, 1900. Frank Lloyd Wright, architect.

Katsura Imperial Villa, Kyoto. Seventeenth century.

Entrance Hall, Gamble House, California, 1908. Greene & Greene, architects.

Interior of rural home (*minka*).

Japanese Influence upon Modern Architecture

The Japanese perception of beauty can also be seen in the concepts of *wabi* (simple quietude) and *sabi* (elegant simplicity). The opposite of gorgeous splendor, these suggest a modest beauty striving for something closer to nature than nature itself. *Wabi*, in particular, evolved as a reaction against the dazzling continental culture imported from China during the sixteenth century. *Wabi* today detects beauty in nonmaterialistic, spiritual freedom and in harmony with nature. At the same time it contains aspects of the philosophy of "less is more" that Ludwig Mies van der Rohe advocated in the modern architectural movement. What attracted the attention of Mies, as well as Walter Gropius and Frank Lloyd Wright, was the concept in Japanese architecture of enclosing a simple structure with a thin membrane to create a composition in which there is a sense of tension in simplicity. There remains, however, one significant point of divergence: modern architecture, along with the expansion of industry, is geared towards an artificial art. What lies at the heart of the Japanese perception of beauty is the desire to reproduce nature, to achieve a fusion with nature, even in architecture, a most unnatural creation.

Unfortunately, this priceless legacy appears to be disappearing. Visitors to Tokyo are often stunned, even disappointed, to find the same skyscrapers that impose themselves on the skyline in New York and Chicago. Of course this is due in part to urbanization, but it may also be related to the growing distance not only between man and nature, but paradoxically, despite the concentration of population, the distance between people.

About this Book

Closeness to nature is the ultimate goal of Japanese architecture. As a result, the Japanese house plan can be described as being composed of three parts: exterior, intermediate, and interior. The exterior is of course symbolized by the garden, and the interior is where the inhabitants spend most of their time. The intermediate area is an important buffer between these two and helps to draw nature into the home while still providing protection and security. The first section of this book looks at this intermediate space which consists of the entranceway, the veranda, and screening devices. The second section describes the elements of interior space, starting with tatami mats and ending with the Japanese bath. By looking at the color and black-and-white plates and sketches, and reading the text, you will be able to pick and choose what appeals to you and remodel your home or apartment with traditional Japanese ideas.

I believe that every country's architectural tradition is unique and contains suggestions for improving the quality of our lives. This book introduces Japan's own unique architectural heritage. I will be very happy if it succeeds in giving you satisfactory results and a better idea of how we Japanese live at home. If, furthermore, through this book an appreciation of the uniqueness of each culture, not just that of the one we are most accustomed to, leads to mutual respect and friendship, I will be doubly happy.

Koji Yagi

INTERMEDIATE SPACE

In the Japanese home, there is no clear demarcation between the interior and the exterior. There is, instead, an intermediate area occupied by three elements: a formal entranceway, a veranda, and various screening devices used in place of Western-style doors and windows. All of these link inner components with outer, and bring nature almost indoors while still shielding man from the elements.

2. A simple wooden veranda serves as an important intermediary between this study and the garden. Bamboo blinds modulate the amount of light and ventilation, and also provide privacy.

3. An inner courtyard shared by all of the rooms in this house gives continuity to the living space, in addition to providing an area for solitary relaxation or an outdoor party.

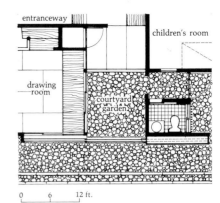

entranceway

children's room

drawing
room

courtyard
garden

0   6   12 ft.

4. A sea of pebbles extending from the garden into the home brings the exterior world into the interior world.

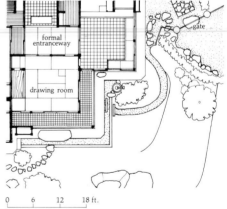

5. Delicate shoji doors are the only barrier here between the interior and exterior. If the shoji are completely removed, nature is immediately drawn into the home, providing a natural source of decoration.

6. The utter simplicity of this veranda belies its perfectly executed function of mediating between two contrasting zones.

7. A few saplings bring nature almost within arm's reach. The sound of gently falling rain or leaves rustling in the wind gives this house the impression of being in the middle of a forest, far away from the cares of the world.

8. Even the materials used for the veranda reveal its mediating role between two diverse zones. The natural wood floors of the veranda complement the color and texture of both the tatami in the living room, and the grass and stones outside.

9. Open corners created upon removing the shoji doors produce a panoramic view of the garden and increase one's viewing pleasure.

10. A modern rendition in steel of bamboo blinds provides privacy for this third-floor apartment in the city.

11. Screened windows provide protection, ventilation, and beauty. The bamboo screens here complement the tatami and wood interior exquisitely.

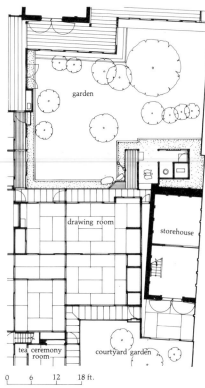

12. The partitioning system skillfully and artistically expands or contracts space according to need. In the summertime, breezes allowed to flow through the house provide natural ventilation.

13. The low, overhanging eaves of the Japanese house protect shoji from rain, and control the flow of light, while also creating a space underneath where one may entertain informally or enjoy a splendid day alone.

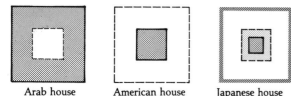

Arab house   American house   Japanese house

Three Types of Enclosures

The Japanese house is surrounded by a "soft" natural barrier.

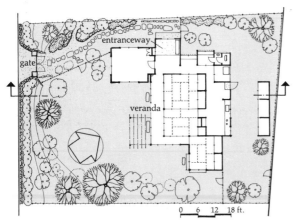

Plan of Japanese house and garden.

INTERMEDIATE SPACE

In the traditional Japanese house, the distinction between interior space and exterior space is not clearly defined. Nature is drawn into the house, rather than excluded from it, by a variety of means such as shoji, bamboo screens, and the entranceway or veranda. Similarly, the interior can be extended beyond the walls of the house with the same devices, as people attempt to live as one with nature.

A comparison of Arab, American, and Japanese house plans will show that the Arab house is constructed around a courtyard, with thick walls built to the edge of the site. In the American suburban house plan, there is often no hedge to designate the boundary. The house, with reinforced doors and windows, is merely surrounded by a lawn. The Japanese house, in contrast, has a hedge around not just the edge of the lot, but the perimeter of the building as well.

The enclosure around the Japanese house is "soft," as opposed to the hard walls of the Arab house, and the open area around the American house. Or, put in another way, the distinction between the public and private areas in the Arab and American plans is clear, and one knows whether one is inside or outside a house, whereas the Japanese house has a certain ambiguity.

Privacy

Although the Japanese house plan may lead to some ambiguity, Japanese architecture nevertheless attempts to protect a certain space from the exterior environment. And vague though it may be, there is still some kind of division between the two zones, determined primarily by whether one is wearing shoes or not.

The feeling that Japanese houses afford little or no privacy is due to the fact that, although the number of barriers is rich in variety, they remain thin and light. But this poses no problem to the Japanese, for there is a certain refinement about a soft, barely perceptible light seeping through a shoji paper door, or the sound of rain just on the other side of a latticed window. The ambiguity about the house is, indeed, pleasant.

In fact, privacy is preserved not physically but through distance, and Japanese refer to the most private part of the house, or the most sacred part of a shrine, as the "deep, inner recess." Unlike Western brick and stone design schemes which call for an interior and exterior consciously divided by walls, a

Cross section.

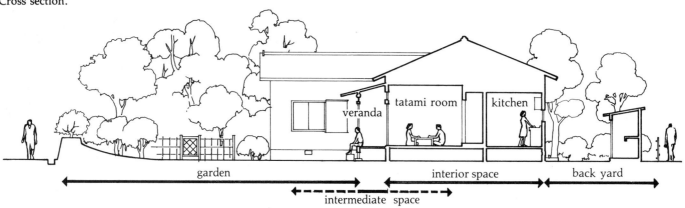

hierarchy of space, as discussed in the Introduction, has emerged in Japan. The open space around the innermost, private bed chamber is divided into several rooms by the use of movable partitions. From this innermost room is a continuum of space through the rest of the house to the area below the eaves, to the garden, and even beyond the garden in some cases when distant scenery is included as part of the overall design.

The Garden

In comparing photographs of Western gardens and Japanese gardens, one notices that in many Western plans the garden is viewed from outside and the building placed against that background. Japanese gardens, on the other hand, are intended to be viewed from an interior space against the background of a wall or fence. This is because Japanese gardens are designed in concert with the room interiors, giving full consideration to sight lines from the rooms, the corridor, or a special viewing platform.

This difference in perspective is indicative of the Japanese concept of the house. In fact, one of the words for family or home in Japanese, *katei*, is a juxtaposition of the characters for "house" and "garden," revealing that the concept of house and garden as a unified whole has existed for quite some time.

The Townhouse Plan

The scarcity of space in Japan has led to interesting variations of the typical house plan. The *machiya*, or "townhouses," of Kyoto, for example, are distinguished by their long, narrow plan. Even in compact areas like these, where houses are only a few inches apart, the harmony between interior and exterior is preserved, and the garden plays a central role. The room closest to the main street is often used for business purposes—goods are displayed and orders taken—so that this area becomes a part of the street, or, conversely, the street becomes a part of the house. The most private room of a *machiya* usually faces a garden. An open corridor connects the main house to a wing where often the first generation lives separately from, but still near, the second generation.

In this way, unity and spaciousness are preserved even in the smallest of spaces, and the needs of people, who are, after all, the focal point of every house, comfortably provided for.

Intermediate Space Components

As previously mentioned, the intermediate space can be seen as an important extension of the house, and as an extension of the garden. The three chapters that follow will talk about three major elements found in this intermediate zone: the formal entranceway, the veranda, and screening devices. The entranceway is where shoes are removed, symbolizing the transition from the exterior to the interior. The veranda is a multipurpose area where one can relax or entertain visitors informally. Screening devices help to unite man and nature by providing ways of allowing the inhabitants of a house to see or hear nature with little difficulty, while still protecting them from the elements.

The intermediate space is an important buffer zone between the interior and exterior.

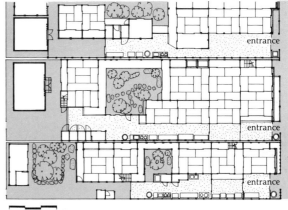

0   6   12   18 ft.

The townhouses (*machiya*) of Kyoto make maximum use of a limited area. (Plan for three houses.)

Exterior of *machiya*.

THE FORMAL ENTRANCEWAY

Shoes are a symbol of the life led outside the home. As we remove them in the entranceway, we enter a different world—the private, personal world of the home.

14. Shoes are removed and left in the entranceway.

15. Flowers and a painting serve as decoration.

16. The stone step separates interior from exterior.

17. In the entranceway begins the Japanese love of wood.

18. The top of the shoe cabinet is ideal for simple displays.

19. Straw cushions and a bench are provided for visitors.

20. An inner garden beckons guests as soon as they enter the home.

21. The view from the entranceway, too, is important.

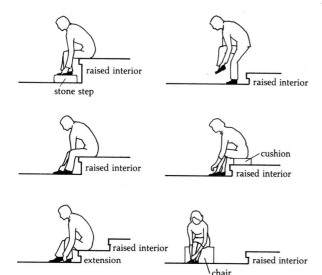

Suggested layouts for entranceway with and without accessories.

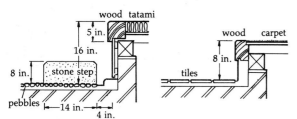

Section of raised interior: (left) with stone step; (right) without stone step.

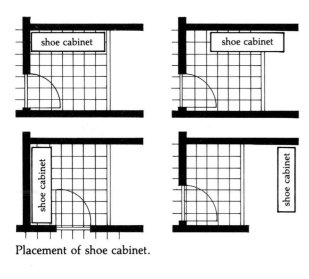

Placement of shoe cabinet.

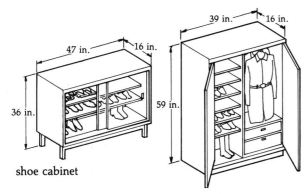

shoe cabinet

closet for shoes, coats, etc.

THE FORMAL ENTRANCEWAY

In contrast to entering the house through the kitchen or the veranda from the garden, the *genkan* is the formal entranceway to the Japanese home. The original religious significance of this word has faded, but as it is here that shoes are removed, this area represents the division between the "unclean" exterior and the "clean" interior. This delineating function is emphasized by the different material used in the entranceway, compared with those used in the exterior and in the interior; by the stone step where shoes are removed; and by the difference in level between the entry at ground level and the raised floor of the interior of the house.

Because land in metropolitan areas such as Tokyo is at such a premium, ceilings in high-rise buildings are often built low to make maximum use of the available space. Thus the difference in level mentioned above may be reduced to only a few inches. Nevertheless the entranceway is an essential part of every house or apartment, and the difference in level is an important visual clue to inform Japanese that this is where shoes are removed before entering the interior.

As a Storage and Display Area

In addition to the stone step and other accessories—such as a cushion or chair that may be used when removing one's shoes—the entranceway in Japan contains a cabinet for all of the shoes belonging to family members and house slippers which they change into. (Visitors' shoes are usually left on the floor, unless they are staying overnight.) Although umbrellas, coats, and hats are also kept here, in the average Japanese house, the shoe cabinet usually retains a separate identity, and the top of it is used as a display area.

The formal entranceway is decorated to symbolize its role as a buffer between interior and exterior, formal and informal, clean and unclean. Yet, since it is a confined space, decoration is kept to a minimum. Should the head of the house have some kind of collection, part of it may be displayed. Alternatively, seasonal flower arrangements may be placed on a small stand, on a fixed shelf, or on top of the shoe cabinet. Shoji, a single-leaf screen (see Pl. 14), or a mere wall will provide an attractive backdrop for the display. Instead of freshly cut flowers, flower boxes, potted plants, or bonsai may be displayed.

Relationship to the Garden

Many Japanese houses are designed so that the garden is visible from the entranceway. These days, when the approach from the road to the house is short, the front garden often ceases to resemble a garden at all. In such cases, visitors will be pleasantly surprised when they catch a glimpse of a courtyard garden from the entranceway. Needless to say, the design of such gardens is subject to considerable variety, but one thing should be kept in mind: the line of vision should be carefully designed so as not to impinge on the privacy of the family.

In the case of a courtyard garden intended primarily for display purposes, special attention should be paid to the background. One may go to considerable pains to create a beautiful scene through the use of bamboo, stones, water, and garden shrubs, but the whole effect may be destroyed if the background is not carefully considered. An earthen or stone wall, or a fence made of wood or bamboo, for example, would be attractive. If the neighboring house stands in the background—and there is little that can be done about that!—a more natural effect can be achieved by hanging a bamboo blind just beyond the garden.

Where only part of the garden, especially the lower section, is visible, one has the advantage of being able to block off direct sunlight and also having more privacy. If the top half of the window or wall is replaced with shoji, a soft light will filter through while the changing seasons can still be observed in the garden through the lower half of the window. In the winter, snow lends to the shoji a beautiful, brilliant whiteness.

Illumination

Since the primary function of the formal entranceway is to provide an area where shoes may be exchanged for house slippers, and an area for subtle decoration, minimal illumination seems more than adequate. Yet in a home where there may be no custom of removing the shoes upon entering the house, it is better that this be made as easy as possible to understand. For example, part of the entranceway beyond the front door may be floored with stone or laid with carpeting from the place where shoes are to be changed, marked by the shoe cabinet and slippers for indoor wear. To further emphasize this special area, a spotlight or a Japanese-style paper lantern may be used with good results. Another spotlight may be used to draw attention to the articles or flower arrangement on display, although here again, a paper lantern creates a lovely Japanese ambience.

Illumination of the garden is also important, especially where the garden is visible from the entranceway. A stone lantern, or a hanging lantern, or a spotlight, either outside or inside, will do very nicely. But in order to best show off the beauty of the garden, the most complementary illumination is created when it is placed at ground level. Whichever form of lighting is used, the brief communion between man and nature will be heightened.

Finishing Touches

It is very common in Japan for visitors to conduct all of their business in the entranceway. Since family members would not be able to relax for the duration of the visit if the interior of the house were open to view, the line of vision from the entranceway to the interior should be blocked off either by a wall, a single-leaf screen, or split curtains (see Pl. 15).

An excellent way to welcome guests is by burning incense in the entranceway just before they arrive. This tradition has virtually disappeared in Japan today, but in the old days, the aristocracy developed exquisite blends of incense, and these were used to express feelings of joy, grief, love, and affection.

Since it is in the formal entranceway that visitors make their first impression of a home, flowers, incense, and a thoughtfully prepared garden view can be used to show one's hospitality and to share the warmth of a household.

ENTRANCEWAY WITH VIEW OF COURTYARD

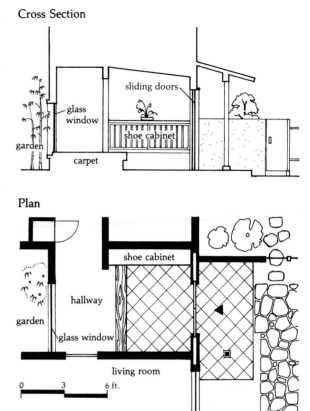

Visual continuity from the garden outside to the courtyard garden inside is achieved in this plan.

ENTRANCEWAY WITH TATAMI

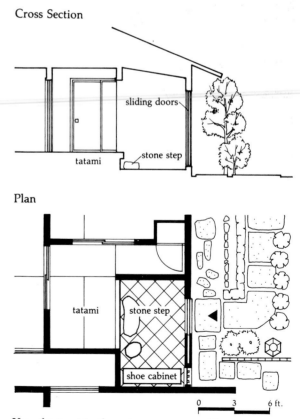

Use of tatami in the entranceway provides textural continuity with tatami used in the rest of the house.

THE VERANDA

The veranda serves as an informal area in which to entertain friends, a place to relax with family members, and a zone where the heat of summer and the cold of winter are ameliorated—besides being the setting for a rendezvous between man and nature.

22. The veranda serves as a comfortable, multi-purpose area.

23. The washbasin and stand are traditional outdoor accessories.

24. Bamboo produces a beautiful, cool veranda.

25. A stone pathway leads one to and from the garden.

26. Wood is most suitable for the veranda.

27. The area under the eaves may serve as a passageway.

28. Even the space under the eaves can be a thing of beauty.

The veranda is a convenient place to relax and enjoy sunshine and fresh air. The large stone in front of the veranda is used when removing one's shoes.

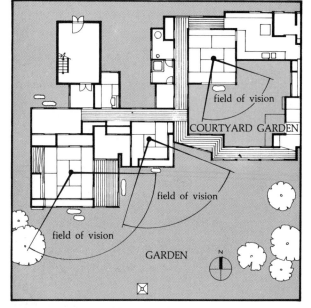

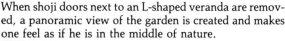

When shoji doors next to an L-shaped veranda are removed, a panoramic view of the garden is created and makes one feel as if he is in the middle of nature.

Heavy wooden shutters provide protection during bad weather, and privacy at night.

In the morning, the shutters are stored away in a closet at the end of the veranda.

THE VERANDA

The veranda (*engawa*) in Japan evolved as the eaves of the house were extended to provide protection for the shoji sliding doors made of paper which face the exterior of the house and which often substitute for solid walls. Heavy wooden shutters, called "rain doors" in Japanese, were also designed, to be used with the shoji as a further means of protection and insulation, and as a crime deterrent. Erected immediately outside the shoji, these rain doors transform the area under the eaves into an extension of the garden. Erected at the edge of the eaves, they make the veranda an even more integral part of the interior as it modulates the area between the inner and outer zones, allowing cool breezes and sunlight into the house, or protecting the home from rain, wind, or even fire.

From the interior, the veranda may in fact be viewed as an extension of floor space, and can even serve when necessary as an informal living area. Conversely, from the outside, since there are usually no railings and it is raised only a few inches above the ground, the veranda may be viewed as a part of the garden.

This difference in level between the veranda and the ground is a major means of demarcating interior space from exterior space in the same way as the step difference in the entranceway. It will be recalled that business is often completely conducted in the entranceway. In a similar way, friends or neighbors may appear at the veranda, keeping their shoes on and remaining on the ground or using the veranda as a bench, while the greeter remains on the veranda, usually seated Japanese-style with legs tucked underneath, and with some tea to share with the visitor. It may be interesting to note that the veranda performed this status-differentiation role as far back as the period of the samurai. Those of the highest rank, for example, would sit in the inner room carpeted with tatami, those next in rank would sit on the veranda, and those of the lowest rank would remain on the ground.

In addition to providing access to the house, or to the garden, the veranda, it must not be forgotten, is a very real transition between two different zones and provides structural continuity. One way in which this is expressed is through the selection of materials. The wood and bamboo used for the veranda contrast in texture and resilience with the materials used in the interior of the house, exemplified by tatami and shoji, and the exterior of stones, grass, and plants.

Construction

To the Japanese, there is a distinct beauty to be detected in the space under the eaves. Since homes in Japan are generally raised about 1 1/2 feet off the ground, the area under the eaves is either elevated to the level of the interior or kept at ground level. When this space is raised to the level—or almost to the level—of the interior, it serves as a veranda and as an extension of the interior, when the shoji or rain doors are removed.

A variation of this finds the transitional space between interior and exterior not limited to the area well shielded from the elements under the eaves, but extended beyond them. Yet another variation extends this area even further, producing what the Japanese poetically call the "moon-viewing dais" which they use to admire the beauty of the moon and the stars, especially in early autumn.

When the space under the eaves is kept at ground level, it assumes the character of part of the garden, but is deliberately designed of stone or gravel, in contrast to the garden, and then serves as a passageway or a terrace. Alternatively, part of the garden may actually be transported into the house and serve as an indoor garden.

In all of these, a combination of shoji, and rain doors made of wood, or glass doors are used to form a boundary between the two zones. Recently there has emerged a vogue for using French windows instead of wooden doors. When these are used at the edge of the eaves, the veranda then becomes a kind of greenhouse. In addition to these various kinds of doors, bamboo or reed screens may be used on sunny days to filter sunlight.

When selecting materials for the veranda, wood with a nice grain is highly recommended since it will produce beautiful results and also provide years of pleasurable viewing. Boards can be placed either lengthwise or laterally, but if placed laterally, wide-sectioned wood creates the best effect. Should the eaves be sufficiently deep, tatami matting may even be used. This lends it a more formal air, and turns the veranda into a kind of corridor or even part of the room to which it is contiguous. Care should be taken that this section does not protrude from beneath the eaves because of the danger of the wood rotting or the tatami becoming discolored through long exposure to sunlight. In such cases, bamboo is probably best, although this virtually precludes the use of chairs and tables. Sitting Japanese-style solves this problem, however, since Japanese cushions may be placed on the floor.

When gravel, stone, or tile is used, as in the case when the veranda is not elevated, the section lying in the direct line of raindrops as they drip off the eaves should be changed or cleaned as, otherwise, the rain leaves behind unsightly marks. A material that is washable with water or a light cleanser is best suited to both the veranda and the area beneath.

To complete your veranda, you may want to provide some outside accessories. The Japanese are given a visual clue of the transition from one zone to the other when they are ready to return to the home after, for example, working in the garden. This visual reminder is the large, often interestingly-shaped, stone placed in front of the veranda where shoes are removed. The removal of shoes, as was discussed earlier, determines for the Japanese the difference between interior and exterior. In addition to this stone, one may also provide a stand with washbasin which, in the past, was placed near the toilet located at the end of the veranda. Today, it may be used for washing hands after gardening.

Handrails are more the exception than the rule to effect the open quality of the veranda. Generally speaking, no furniture is placed on the veranda since it can double as a bench to sit on, a table on which to serve refreshments or to lay clothes for mending, or an open crib for a baby. Shoes are not worn when the veranda is above ground level.

VERANDA VARIATIONS

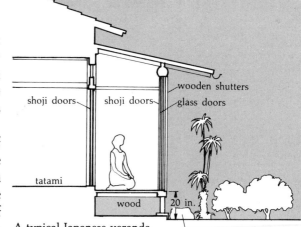
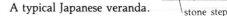

A typical Japanese veranda.

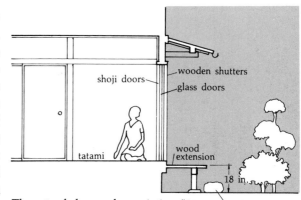

The extended veranda, variation #1.

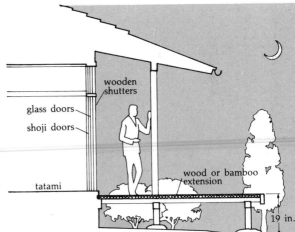

The extended veranda, variation #2. Referred to in Japanese as the "moon-gazing dais."

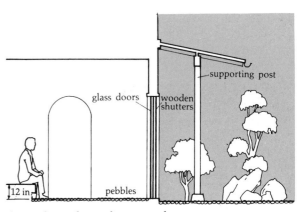

An unelevated, receding veranda.

SCREENING DEVICES

Used in place of or in addition to walls and windows, these devices combine function with beauty by providing light, ventilation, and privacy in pleasing ways.

29. Screens and windows go together well.

30. Screens provide some privacy from neighbors.

31. Screens also provide protection from the sun.

32. Split curtains are a novel way to advertise the name of a shop.

33. Vision, but not ventilation, is inhibited by split curtains.

34. Bamboo grid window with shoji backing.

35. Window with bamboo latticework.

36. Heavy wood latticing and reed screens.

37. Shoji with latticework.

38. Attractive in the daytime.

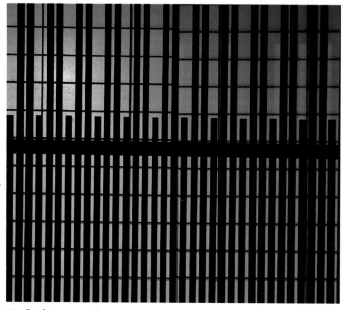
39. Striking at night.

29

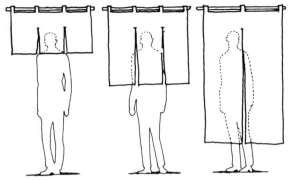

Noren may be made into any shape or size.

HOW TO MAKE YOUR OWN NOREN

Measure width of door or corridor. Decide length. Buy appropriate amount of fabric (taking into consideration seam allowance), thread, and curtain rod. Cut out main body and loop sections, matching any horizontal pattern or design. Join sides of section A to B, and B to C, by stitching 6 inches down from top of each section. Press seam allowance open. Finish edges of main body and loops by turning raw edges under twice and slipstitching or machine stitching. Corners may be mitered if desired. Fold loops in half lengthwise, right sides together, and stitch. Press seam open and then turn right side out. Turn raw edges under. Fold loops in half and place main body of curtain so that 1 inch is between layers. Position rightmost and leftmost loops flush with edges of main body. Center other two loops on seams. Machine stitch or hand sew loops to main body, bearing in mind weight of curtain and diameter of curtain rod. (Note: The pattern below is for a 35-inch doorway.)

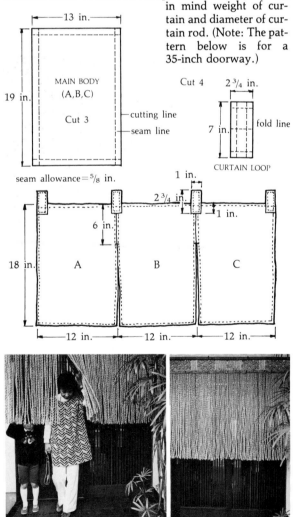

Noren may also be made of strands of hemp, which customers push aside as they enter or leave a shop.

SCREENING DEVICES

The hot and sultry Japanese summer is unpleasant to say the least. The cold of winter can be overcome by simply putting on more clothing or turning on the heat, but the only ways to resist heat and humidity are by blocking out the sun's rays and allowing the unfettered passage of air. It is for this reason that Japanese architecture favors a minimum of walls and the use of furniture that can be easily moved to create an open-air style. Although this leads to a loss of visual privacy, there are several means of mitigating this loss while still providing optimal air circulation and obstructing the sun's rays.

Split Curtains

Noren are ungathered split curtains made of cloth or hemp which were used as shades in front of homes as far back as the Heian period. Much later they came to replace the doors of large shops to allow the easy passage of customers. Today they continue this tradition primarily for drinking and eating establishments serving Japanese food.

In addition to providing unusual advertising space for a particular enterprise by displaying the shop's name, trademark, and specialty, *noren* are used to indicate when a place is open for business. If no *noren* can be seen, or if the *noren* are still behind the door, the establishment is not yet open.

In the home, *noren* serve as attractive space dividers. They are often hung to block viewing into the kitchen or some other private area from the formal entranceway or from the passageway.

Of all the forms of screening deployed in Japanese interior design, the *noren* is the softest. Not only is the material soft, but the way in which it is used creates a soft, gentle effect. Since it flutters in the breeze, the *noren* enables one to "see" the wind, and, when used in conjunction with wind chimes that enable one to "hear" the wind, it is really as though one is "experiencing" the wind. This produces a particularly refreshing feeling during the hot summer months.

The fact that one has to touch the *noren* before passing through lends it not only a visual but also a tactile appeal. In fact, the Japanese feel no displeasure at brushing the *noren* with their heads as they pass through an entranceway. This, however, may be an unfamiliar custom for others, and, since there are times when one's hair may become disheveled, care should be taken in selecting the most appropriate place and height for *noren*.

Bamboo Screens

The *sudare* screen is knotted together from strips of bamboo, and is not as soft as the *noren* curtain. Consequently, it is rarely used in corridors. As it can be raised or lowered to a desired height, it was originally used as a blind. While the *noren* may flutter in the breeze, it nevertheless totally restricts visibility, whereas the *sudare*, as a non-opaque screen, is effective on bright days in allowing those inside to see out while preventing those outside from seeing in. However, in case the scenery is distracting, all one has to do is position oneself far enough from the *sudare* to solve the problem.

The *sudare* is usually hung at the edge of the eaves of the veranda or on the outside of windows where, by carefully adjusting the height to which it is unrolled and tied, it can be used to provide relief from the sun's glare. Furthermore, in our modern residential blocks, it also affords residents much-needed visual protection from the neighboring house. And since one of the characteristics of Japanese garden landscaping is that everything—from moss and stones to garden shrubs—is designed to be appreciated from a low angle, the top half of a window can be covered with a *sudare* without impairing appreciation of the garden.

Other possibilities include hanging a *sudare* on the wall and using it as a frame for a scroll or painting. If your home has shoji doors, these may be removed and then replaced with several *sudare* in the summer. *Sudare* may also be placed in upright frames and made into a folding room divider.

Marsh Reed Screens

The *yoshizu* is similar to the *sudare*, but differs in that whereas the *sudare* is regulated vertically, the *yoshizu* is drawn from left to right horizontally. It is thus often used in corridors to protect rooms from the heat of the sun. Like the *sudare*, it is easily moved or changed, and so ideally suited to shop facades or rooms that receive the light and heat of the sun for only a limited period each day.

The *yoshizu* can be used to provide protection from the sun by being designed into a kind of pergola. Alternatively it can be used as a fence for the home or garden. In multiple-story apartment blocks, the *yoshizu* may be fixed to the guardrail on the balcony to provide visual protection as well as a backdrop for a little garden. Like *sudare*, *yoshizu* may also be placed in a frame and made into a folding room divider or a beautiful sliding door. It may be used for cupboard doors in the kitchen or the garage or the bathroom.

Propped up against the veranda, *yoshizu* may be used as a temporary shelter for equipment or a makeshift playhouse for children. It may also provide shade for a vegetable patch.

Latticework

The aforementioned screening devices, while allowing the passage of air and providing sufficient visual protection, failed in the old days to provide protection against theft. The solution was the development of wooden lattices. Although not as sturdy as iron lattices, the wooden variety found in Japan provided adequate security as well as another source of interior decoration, especially in contrast to white shoji doors and natural-colored walls.

If the latticed screen is badly deployed, the protective quality is emphasized. It is thus best deployed as an internal partition (for which a wide lattice is recommended). Alternatively, it may be deployed as mere decoration. A more unusual use is to create a stairway effect of lattice and hang this between the kitchen and the living room. Thin latticework, like the *sudare* and *yoshizu*, offer numerous possibilities for the kitchen, bedroom, and bathroom.

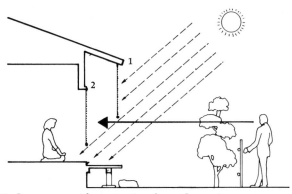

1. Screens provide protection from the sun's rays.
2. They can also prevent people on the outside from looking into the home, while permitting those inside to look out.

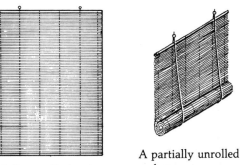

A fully unrolled *sudare*.

A partially unrolled *sudare*.

Sudare are approximately 35 inches wide, and come in small, medium, and large sizes.

Reed screens may be propped up against the roof of the veranda during the hottest time of the day.

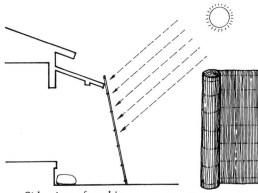

Side view of *yoshizu*.

Yoshizu may be rolled up when not in use and are easy to carry.

INTERIOR SPACE

Japanese interior space is a study in simplicity and flexibility. Tones are quiet, and materials, wherever possible, natural. Translucent and opaque sliding doors and a variety of portable partitions give the living space a wonderful versatility by providing an effortless and tasteful way of altering the size and shape of a room.

41. Shoji panels and tatami mats are quintessential elements of Japanese interior design.

42. The ease with which shoji and tatami may be used to transform any room is but only one attractive feature of Japanese interior decorating. The simple alcove with a modern painting consummates this composition.

43. A typical interior plan consists of an alcove for modest displays and a low, portable table. Cushions should be brought out for guests, but family members feel no compunction about sitting or lying directly on the tatami. If the shoji doors are removed, the interior space expands to include the veranda and the few pieces of furniture on it.

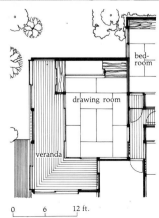

bed-room

drawing room

veranda

0   6   12 ft.

44. The austere elegance of a Japanese-style room may at first be jolting but has a tranquilizing effect as, within seconds, the harried soul quietly winds down.

45. A minimum of decoration leads one to appreciate the intrinsic beauty of this room.

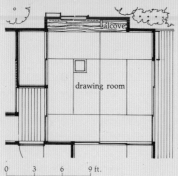

46. Awareness of the seasons is central to Japanese aesthetics and architecture. In these four plates, four different moods are expressed through changing the decoration in the alcove.

New Year's is the most special season for the Japanese and requires traditional adornment. Here, long strands of young willow, accented with camellias, cascade from a bright green bamboo container. The scroll with red sun and Mount Fuji is a particularly auspicious combination, as are the red and white color of the paper napkins underneath the incense burner.

47. Spring is a time to welcome the rebirth of nature after a long, cold winter. The Dolls' Festival on March 3 is celebrated here with shocking pink peach blossoms and a scroll decorated with exquisite handmade paper dolls. Candles placed in bamboo and washi paper baskets provide illumination.

48. Summer in Japan is announced by the burst of greenery as warm rains bathe the country. Removal of the shoji panel behind the screened window, and a cool flower arrangement produce a light, refreshing atmosphere.

49. Autumn is cherished by the Japanese for the all too brief period of brilliant foliage followed quickly by the quiet, melancholy tones of nature preparing for the winter ahead. This is a time to reflect upon the irrevocable passage of time and the beauty of Japanese traditions.

50. With only shoji and tatami, one can blend East and West with unquestionably satisfying results. The delicate shoji doors contrast splendidly with the solid wood table, and the use of tatami, in addition to the rug, to adorn the beautiful natural wood floor is masterful.

51. Shoji, a hallmark of Japanese interior design, goes well with any decor. Here it handsomely complements the leather furniture, glass-top coffee table, brass chandelier, and beige carpeting.

53. By simply raising the level of one half of this room and laying tatami down with a few cushions, a Japanese-style living space is easily created. The kitchen is in the other half of this room.

52. Displaying its marvelous adaptability, the shoji in this room responds beautifully to the natural wood floor and ceiling and wood furniture.

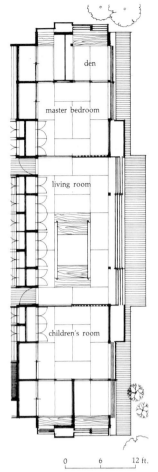

den

master bedroom

living room

children's room

0   6   12 ft.

54. When the sliding doors here are opened, one large room is created; when closed, three rooms. The black wallpaper of the doors accentuates both the partitioning and the unifying function of the sliding doors, besides serving as a striking backdrop for flower arrangements and paintings.

55. This room is quickly and easily transformed into a guest room, complete with its own garden, upon closing the sliding doors. Bedding for guests is stored in the closet area next to the tatami. (For a close-up of the study, see Pl. 60.)

56. A split-level arrangement gives this living room an unusual versatility. Guests may be entertained either in the lower zone furnished with chairs, or the upper zone furnished with tatami and cushions. In addition, the plain wood ledge just beyond the tatami may be transformed into a bench and used with either zone.

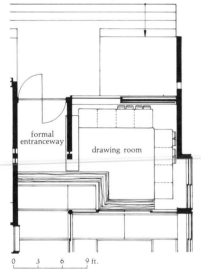

formal
entranceway

drawing room

0   3   6   9 ft.

57. The multi-purpose potential of tatami is particularly suitable for a cabin in the mountains. The area laid with tatami here may be used for eating, sleeping, writing letters—whatever you wish.

INTERRELATIONSHIP OF HOUSE COMPONENTS

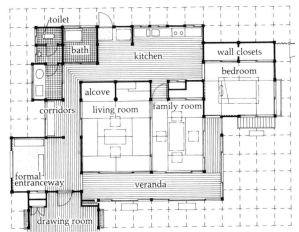

Through this grid pattern superimposed on a house plan, one can see that the major components of a Japanese house are interrelated in design. The size of one grid is approximately 3 ft. × 3 ft. Typical dimensions for the following items show how this interrelationship works:

Tatami (1 mat) = 3 ft. × 6 ft.
Alcove = 3 ft. by 6 ft.
Wall closet = 3 ft. × 6 ft.
Bath = 6 ft. × 6 ft.
Toilet = 3 ft. × 4½ or 6 ft. (width)
Veranda = 3, 4½, or 6 ft. (width)
Corridor = 3 or 4½ ft. (width)
Fusuma = 3 ft. × 6 ft.
Shoji = 3 ft. × 6 ft.
Wooden shutters = 3 ft. × 6 ft.

Out of the fitted wall closet comes a variety of furniture and other everyday items.

Bedding (*futon*) is removed from the closet and placed on the floor.

INTERIOR SPACE

In the Western house, the functions of rooms—dining, living, and bed—are clearly defined. In the traditional Japanese house, one room can have several functions. The function, and size as well, of a room is determined by usage, and since needs change through the course of the day, one Japanese-style room can act as several of its Western equivalent.

How is this done? This unique system is related to the concept of space in Japanese architecture. Since the roof of a Japanese wood-frame house is supported on pillars, not walls, partitioning does not imply something solid or permanent. The development of movable partitioning such as sliding doors and folding screens evolved in response to this innovative perception of space, and rooms are altered effortlessly and quickly with these in the Japanese house. Rooms in the West, in comparison, are appended one by one and separated from each other by solid walls.

The Japanese idea of setting up a room by surrounding a certain space with movable partitioning and furniture enables the function of a given space to be changed by adding, removing, or redistributing pieces of furniture. As a result, there is an interrelationship of design between the floor, pillars, partitioning devices, and furniture. Just as the size of the brick was originally determined by the size of the human hand, so the size of the Japanese house is gauged in terms of human measurements. The tatami mat, originally designed to accommodate one sleeping person or two standing people, continues to be used today to conceptualize the size of a room, so that even amateurs can try their hand at designing their own home.

Partitioning may be totally removed to create one large room out of two or more rooms to accommodate a large number of guests, thanks to this efficient and ingenious system. Such flexibility is useful not only in accommodating large numbers or changing the function of a room, but also in coping with the contrasting lifestyles occasioned by the Japanese summer and winter. In summer, rooms may be "opened" and cross ventilation provided by removing partitioning and creating a large room. In winter, by reducing the size of a room, the area to be heated may be controlled and energy consumption reduced.

Where's the Furniture?

A sophisticated partitioning system is easy enough to understand, but why do Japanese homes give the impression of simplicity and, sometimes, emptiness? First of all, the custom of sitting on the floor (see pp. 64–67) and the use of tatami as a kind of chair, table, and bed lead to an economy of furniture. Next, what little furniture there is is stored away in a fitted wall closet found in every room, and articles for use are removed as needed. For example, at the end of the day, *futon* mattresses, pillows, and blankets are brought out and laid on the tatami floor. Then in the morning, these are returned to the closet and the room is rearranged for use by the family. When it comes to mealtime, a low table and cushions are produced. After the meal is over, the table is cleared, and the family may spend the rest of the evening in the same room watching television.

The wall closet is not particularly noticeable to those unfamiliar with it because it is in effect a kind of opaque sliding door (*fusuma*) and blends in with the rest of the decor. (See Pls. 55, 57, 76.) In fact, the designs found on the larger sliding doors used to partition rooms, and the doors to these closets, are often coordinated.

These days Japanese houses are a combination of Japanese- and Western-style rooms. The Western-style room is usually carpeted and furnished with desks, chairs, cabinets, stereo systems, etc. In contrast, furniture and decoration in the Japanese-style room are kept to a bare minimum. The tatami in the room gives it a somewhat formal air so that it is often reserved for use as a drawing room, a guest room, or, as will be discussed later, a kind of retreat within the home. For many Japanese, a simple, uncluttered tatami room does wonders for the soul.

Natural Colors, Natural Materials

The raw materials used in Japanese architecture give rooms quiet, subdued tones. In principle, the floor is laid with tatami of fragrant, light green rush; walls are made of paper (when, for example, shoji are used), wood, or natural-colored clay; and the ceiling constructed of wood or bamboo. Colors tend to be white or light brown; materials are organic; and texture, matt as opposed to gloss.

It is generally held that materials should be deployed in as natural a manner as possible. Paint is thus seldom used. Fortunately, however, and depending on the life span of the material, paper, even tatami, may be replaced and earthen surfaces redaubed. Since wooden buildings can be renovated bit by bit, the life span of the Japanese house can be several hundred years, and the idea of replacing parts, instead of the whole, pervades traditional Japanese attitudes toward building construction.

A Simple Plan for any Home

Construction of a Japanese corner in one's own home need not be just an idle dream or the task of a professional. Here are some suggestions. First, pick a corner and lay two or more tatami down. Then divide off this space by experimenting with the different kinds of partitions suggested in the following chapters. Bear in mind that the arrangement need not be permanent and that seasonal changes may require alteration. The simplest method is to partition off this area by use of screens. Alternatively, a kind of shoji may be suspended from the ceiling.

A more complicated, but more authentic, method is to erect pillars in four corners and insert either shoji or lattice sliding doors. If possible, raise the level of the Japanese-style room about 12–16 inches above the rest of the house. In this way, a visual clue to remove one's shoes will be provided, and the Japanese atmosphere emphasized. Later, install a Japanese-style alcove where different objects—a flower arrangement, some pottery, a Japanese sword, a little *tansu*, a scroll—may be admired. Add a low table and some cushions made of Japanese fabric, serve sushi with hot sake or sake on the rocks, and relax and enjoy a bit of Japan right at home.

The same space can be used for eating,

entertaining visitors,

studying,

and sleeping.

TATAMI MATS

Tatami mats provide a unique and sensuous kind of flooring. They may be used for sitting, sleeping, or walking on, or, for something novel, as a refreshing covering for tables, benches, and even beds.

58. Tatami borders can impart a sense of direction.
59. New tatami smell like fresh hay.

60. A tatami bed.

61. A tatami dining set.

63. Tatami benches.

62. Borderless half-tatami mats.

64. A tatami dais.

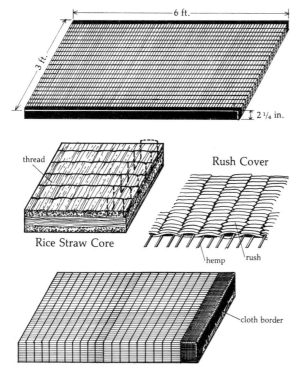

Tatami are made of a tightly-packed core, a rush cover, and two cloth borders.

Detail of core.   Detail of cover.

Decorated *goza* mat.

HOW TO INSTALL TATAMI

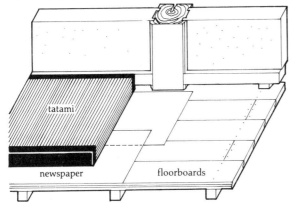

Newspapers or plastic sheets are placed between the floorboards and tatami to reduce dampness.

TATAMI MATS

In the Japanese home tatami mats are used as a surface for sitting, sleeping, and walking on. Light enough to be carried by an adult, mats are composed of a thick rice straw core, a soft reed cover, and two borders of cloth or synthetic tape which protect the sides. Tatami are approximately 3 feet by 6 feet, about the size of a single bed, and $1\,^3/_4$–$2\,^1/_2$ inches thick.

Tatami evolved over a long period, first beginning as a thin, easily folded straw mat on which people sat or slept. Later, more layers of rice straw were added to the core for comfort. A new function of these fortified, but still portable, mats was to indicate differences in rank, the most exalted members being given the privilege of sitting on tatami while others sat on the wooden floor. Tatami eventually came to cover the entire floor and are now a standard item in Japanese-style rooms.

Layout
"A standing person takes up half a mat; a sleeping person, a full mat." As this saying suggests, a single tatami mat accommodates two standing people; thus if two mats are placed together, there is just enough room to seat four to six people around a small table. Since this is perfect for playing cards or for doing flower arrangements, an initial purchase of two mats is recommended. More mats can be added later, following the patterns suggested on the following page.

When it comes to laying several tatami down together, one has to take into account the way in which they reflect light. Since the rushes used for the cover are not very long, they are wound laterally across the width of the mat in close parallel lines. The reflection of light varies according to the placement of the mats. Thus, some tatami will appear light, and others, dark, in the same room. The interesting patterns created add to the attractiveness of tatami.

Tatami provide a convenient way of estimating the size of an apartment or house in Japan. What is decided at the planning stage is the number of mats per room—$4\,^1/_2$, 6, 8, etc.—and the area of each room is subsequently referred to by this number, for example, a six-mat room, an eight-mat room, and so on. In real estate advertisements, the scale of an apartment or house is indicated in this way, providing one with a good idea of size and layout. Despite its importance in the Japanese conception of space, however, tatami are not the module for building proportions as is widely misinterpreted, and in fact, there are a number of "standard" sizes, as well as the practice of tailoring tatami to the available floor space.

In addition to tatami there is also available just the soft reed cover which forms the top layer of tatami. Called *goza*, these can be used in the home to create a tatami-like atmosphere or outside as beach mats.

Ideas
So far we have only looked at tatami as something to sit on. But, originally, tatami placed on top of the floorboards formed a surface which was raised one level above the rest of the floor. A relic of this is seen in the tatami alcove (see Pls. 87, 91, 99)

where a small tatami platform, one or two mats high, is constructed in the corner of a room, on which flower arrangements or pottery can be exhibited. In this way tatami can be used either as a Japanese-style floor or as a display platform.

By piling two or three tatami on top of each other, a bench can be created. This novel use of tatami may have been first used during the Edo period (1615–1868). In 1857, on the occasion of his audience with the shogun, the then American consul, Townsend Harris, found himself perplexed as to whether he should or should not take off his shoes, and whether or not he should sit on the floor. In the end, Harris changed into a new pair of shoes at the entrance, and thus became the first and last person ever to enter Edo castle with his shoes on. The shogun, for his part, was seated upon seven tatami piled on top of each other. The height of this, about 16 inches, was roughly the same as that of an ordinary chair.

This kind of tatami chair or bench, still novel today, can be converted into a low table to be used with a small stool. Should one decide to use tatami this way, the ideal height would be about 12–18 inches. It is advisable to add a wooden frame or some kind of border to protect the edges from fraying. When used as a kind of bench, small flat cushions should be placed on it; when converted into a desk, the use of a tray is recommended. These not only help to protect the tatami but also add a decorative element.

In Japan there is the notion that tatami are to be used only inside the house. It is not, however, absolutely necessary to confine their use to the interior. It is possible, for example, to use tatami, instead of wood or bamboo, for the veranda, or outside on the lawn as a platform for a picnic or an outdoor concert.

Tatami can be used to floor a mobile home or camper. They can then be carried outside and used as mats or as a substitute for beds. In fact, in the past, trains and ships in Japan had sections provided with tatami for the comfort of passengers.

Care and Maintenance
Tatami are surprisingly durable and easy to clean, requiring only a damp cloth or vacuum cleaner with a special brush attachment. Shoes or even house slippers are not worn on tatami, and furniture with slatted or barred legs is recommended to prevent marks from being made on the tatami. It should be noted that tatami are neither fire-resistant nor stain-resistant.

In most homes tatami are aired and dried out once a year in the spring. The straw core will last for many years, but the outer reed will need to be changed every few years by a professional tatami-maker.

Although tatami may be used outside, there is one point about which care should be taken: if exposed to sunlight, they will turn yellow. Furthermore, the straw and rushes will shrink, eliminating the layers of air inside, and begin to mold if tatami become too damp. Thus it is important to bring the tatami indoors after use. This has become less of a problem recently, since the use of a polystyrene filling has made tatami more moisture-resistant, but care should be taken nevertheless.

WAYS TO USE TATAMI

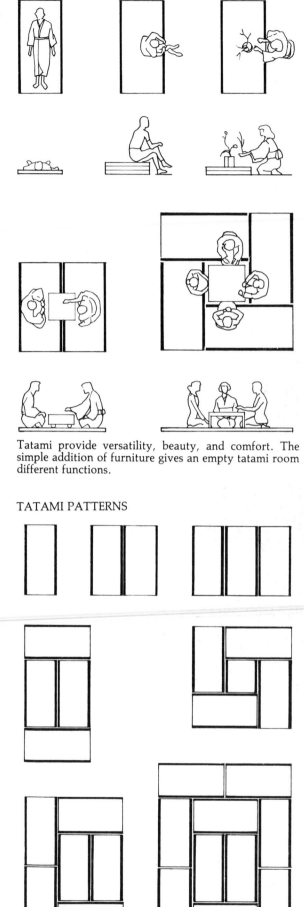

Tatami provide versatility, beauty, and comfort. The simple addition of furniture gives an empty tatami room different functions.

TATAMI PATTERNS

T-shaped patterns are common but + patterns are avoided because of the difficulty in achieving a good fit.

TRANSLUCENT SLIDING DOORS

Shoji serve as a principal partitioning device, in addition to providing a source of exquisite illumination and decoration.

65. Patterns of light and shade give shoji a special beauty.

66. Shoji permit one to control the view from a window.

67. The design possibilities of shoji are delightfully infinite.

68. Creativity is possible even in traditional shoji doors.

69. Movable sections within shoji panels allow one to compose one's own landscape.

70. Shoji serve as a beautiful and ingenious frame for any kind of scene and . . .

71. any kind of day.

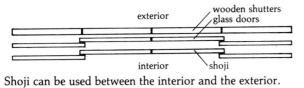

PARTITIONING FUNCTION OF SHOJI

exterior · wooden shutters / glass doors

interior · shoji

Shoji can be used between the interior and the exterior.

room A

room B · shoji

Shoji can be used to separate one room from another.

SHOJI CONSTRUCTION

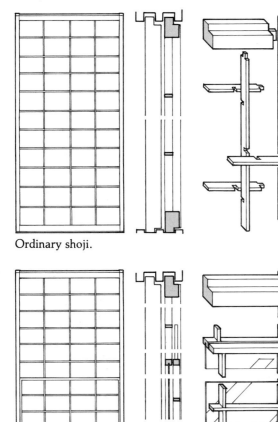

Ordinary shoji.

Shoji with vertical-moving section.

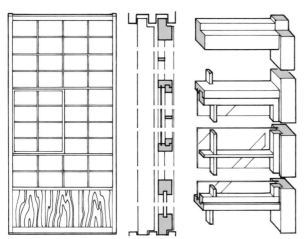

Shoji with horizontal-moving section.

TRANSLUCENT SLIDING DOORS

While tatami will provide a refreshing, sensuous carpeting, shoji sliding doors will transform instantly and beautifully the mood of a home.

Shoji were originally introduced to Japan from China. In China, however, houses were constructed with heavy walls, and shoji were used simply to partition off areas within the interior itself. The basic structural element of Japanese houses, in contrast, are pillars, and shoji had to be employed not only for interior partitioning but also for marking the boundary between interior and exterior. The characteristic paper shoji thus came into existence in response to the need for a partition that admits light, but not drafts.

Construction

Besides their striking beauty, shoji are very light. They are made of a simple skeleton of thin wooden strips arranged in various rectangular patterns and framed by somewhat wider strips, over which paper is usually pasted. The wooden strips are notched into each other from alternate sides to give strength to the frame. The lower portion of the shoji is often a wood panel.

Well-dried, soft, white wood is best for the frame. (Hard wood is more difficult to work with.) The top and bottom of the frame must be prepared with protruding ridges, as shown, in order for the shoji to slide in its runners. The bottom runner need be only 1/8 inch deep, but the top runner should be about 5/8 inch to allow the shoji to be conveniently inserted and removed. To insert the shoji, first incline it a little, and then gently push the upper frame into its runner. The lower frame can then be dropped into place. Wax may be applied to reduce friction.

Japanese shoji paper is traditionally used for the screen itself, though other materials are also acceptable. Because relatively long fibers are used, the texture of Japanese paper is somewhat coarse. This has the effect of diffusing the light that passes through it, creating a generally soft atmosphere. As light conditions change through the course of the day, so, too, does the quality of light created by shoji, and the gentle patterns produced are a joy to watch.

Since the paper "breathes," ventilation is not impeded when shoji doors are closed. Heat loss, on the other hand, appears to be minimal.

Usually the paper is put onto the outside of the shoji, so that the beautiful wood latticework can be seen from inside the room. Should it be desired to have the lattice visible from both sides, rather more elaborate handiwork is necessary, since a double frame must be constructed. On the other hand, should one want both sides of the shoji to be papered, it is a simple matter to apply paper to the two sides of the frame.

Before glass became widely available, sliding wooden shutters were placed outside the shoji for protection, and at night or at times of strong wind or rain, these would be closed. Although the shoji could be left open on hot days, during cold spells they had to be kept shut, preventing people indoors from looking outside or into the garden. The advent of glass provided a solution. One method was to incorporate glass in a portion of the

50

shoji behind the paper. By making that part of the shoji movable, it became possible to see outside without allowing the cold air in, and this kind of shoji came to be called "snow-viewing shoji" (*yukimi-shoji*). When making this kind of shoji, one must bear in mind that the line of vision will be determined by whether people will be sitting on the floor or on chairs.

Applications

For the American home, there are infinite possibilities for incorporating shoji. Shoji may be used like a curtain simply to control the amount of light entering a room by installing them next to regular glass windows. Being similar to double glazing, this arrangement provides good insulation.

Installing shoji over a window is another possibility. In cases where it is difficult to make shoji that fit nicely into the existing window frame, one shoji may be instead suspended from above, or fixed onto the wall, as described on pp. 74–75. This kind of suspended shoji can be used in other ways inside the home. For example, it may be hung as a screen between the dining and living areas, and if a plant or flower arrangement is then placed in front of it, the completely white background provided by the shoji can make it look like a painting. Seen from the other side of the room, it appears as a beautiful silhouette.

If the usual pair of sliding shoji are placed within the perimeter of a window, it is possible to have only half of it open at any time, but if the shoji frame is extended and only one shoji inserted, it becomes possible to have the entire window open. The frame joints must of course be at perfect right angles, and the sides parallel; otherwise it will not match well with the window.

When a window has an unpleasant view, shoji placed over it will be a vast improvement. Walls may also be covered with shoji to increase the sense of spaciousness as well as to add more light through the natural reflecting qualities of shoji. Shoji skylights will add a novel effect to any room and provide just the right amount of light for certain indoor plants.

Shoji has possibilities for the bathroom and the bedroom—for example, a pair of shoji sliding doors for the bath, and several shoji doors for a large closet.

Outside, shoji can provide a lovely enclosure for the veranda. Frosted glass is an excellent substitute for shoji paper. The simple latticework pattern and the opaque milky-white color provide a stunning combination. The insertion of polystyrene, or some other white insulating material, though slightly impairing the translucent quality of the screen, renders the heat retention all the more effective.

Shoji can also be used for a boundary fence if it is fitted with strong white plastic instead of paper.

Care and Maintenance

Shoji are traditionally completely refurbished with new paper just before the New Year's festivities. Holes or rents can be patched with square bits of shoji paper, or, if one wants to be more artistic, with designs of cherry blossoms. Stains or discolorations may require repapering a larger section of the frame.

SHOJI VARIATIONS

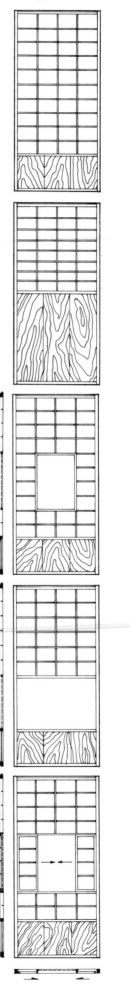
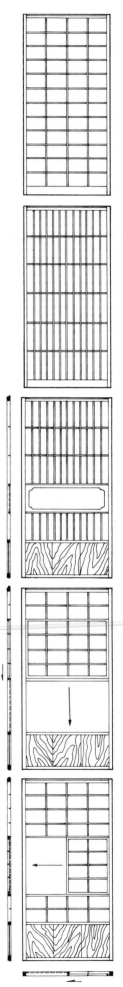

OPAQUE SLIDING DOORS/ TRANSOMS/PORTABLE PARTITIONS

In addition to shoji, there are a number of other partitioning devices which give flexibility to the overall plan.

72. Folding screens as wall decoration.

73. Painted sliding doors.

74. Folding screens used as a room partition.

75. Undecorated sliding doors.

76. Wallpapered sliding doors.

77. Sliding doors with shoji panel.

78. Sliding doors with reed screening.

79. Transom with young bamboo.

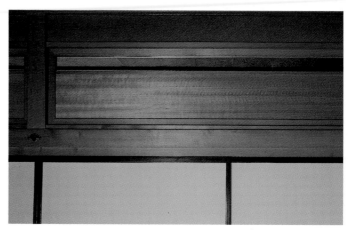

80. Transom with wood paneling.

81. Transom with openwork design.

82. Transom with colored paper.

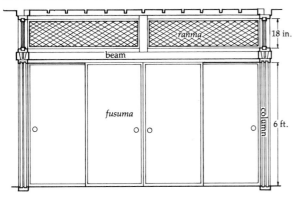

FUSUMA CONSTRUCTION

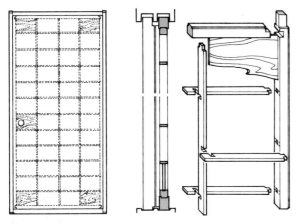

FUSUMA VARIATIONS

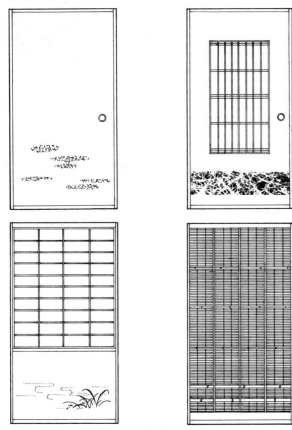

Most *fusuma* are decorated with simple designs. *Fusuma* may also be made with shoji to provide light, and with *yoshizu* to provide ventilation.

OPAQUE SLIDING DOORS/ TRANSOMS/PORTABLE PARTITIONS

Opaque Sliding Doors

Opaque sliding doors (*fusuma*) are used, as a general rule, to divide Japanese-style rooms with tatami from each other, and are removed when occasion demands to make a large reception area. The primary function of shoji, on the other hand, is to divide interior from exterior, and also, in modern Japanese houses with both Japanese- and Western-style rooms, to partition off the places where house slippers are worn—the Western-style rooms and the hallway—from the tatami rooms where house slippers are not worn.

Fusuma, like shoji, consist of a wooden grid frame, but whereas shoji usually have white translucent paper attached to only one side, *fusuma* have a cloth or opaque paper covering on both sides. It is necessary to first apply several sheets of paper as a foundation, but since this is time-consuming, the recent trend has been to fix a sheet of plywood to each side and then put the final surface on.

With shoji, the frame is deliberately left unfinished to enhance the beautiful white shoji paper, but with *fusuma*, colored materials are often used to complement the color and design of the paper or cloth. Black is commonly used; browns, reds, and other dark colors are also popular. But if a plain wood surround is desired, straight-grained wood is best.

If *fusuma* are thought of simply as a movable wall or as large sliding doors, their potential uses are numerous. Cork or steel plate may be used for the surface instead of paper or cloth to produce a bulletin board. Similarly, if the walls or doors of a child's room are made *fusuma*-style, they can be used for drawing pictures on. In fact, Japanese painters often use *fusuma* as a kind of canvas, and a single continuous picture or depictions of the changing seasons will extend across several panels. In the past, visitors were even encouraged to leave poetry behind on the *fusuma* to commemorate the occasion.

A possible modification to the *fusuma* is to replace part of it with shoji or *sudare* or *yoshizu* screens. The shoji section will allow light to penetrate to a back room, while the *sudare* or *yoshizu* section will improve ventilation.

Since the Japanese-style floor is laid with tatami, it is not at all strange to have the runners for sliding doors in the middle of it. If, however, runners are difficult to make or would be unsightly, shoji or *fusuma* can be suspended from the ceiling. By fixing a curtain rail onto the ceiling, a *fusuma* or similar screen could be hung from it when necessary, while it could also be used for hanging an ordinary curtain or a tapestry.

Transoms

The usual height of shoji or *fusuma* is about six feet, which leaves a little space between the upper runner and the ceiling. This space is often filled with a small shoji or *fusuma* panel, latticework, or openwork carving, and is referred to as the *ranma*. In contrast with the fanlight or rose-window found in churches in the West, the *ranma* came to be designed in conjunction with the shoji and *fusuma* in a rectangular frame to be admired from both sides, while improving air circulation and providing light.

In the days before electric lighting, rooms were dim even during the day, so the light coming through a *ranma* with openwork carving, for example, produced a beautiful silhouette effect. There are many kinds of designs one can use to create this interplay of light and shadow, though these days rooms may be too bright for the creation of such silhouettes. One possibility is utilizing a *ranma* design as a bedside lamp shade. It is not necessary to use a wood carving for this; a motif of a flower or a bird, for example, cut into a piece of cardboard, framed, and illuminated from behind is just as effective. Similarly, you may want to make a Japanese-style lamp (see pp. 76–77) with a *ranma* pattern that you have designed yourself.

Portable Partitions

FOLDING SCREENS. There are several types of screens which can be set up and moved about with freedom, one example being the *byobu*. Made up of two or more *fusuma*-like screens joined together, it can stand independently, in a V or W shape, and is easily stored away when not in use. If the front and back are decorated with different colors and patterns, the *byobu* can be turned around every now and then for variety, and serve as a versatile room divider and decorative element.

Being portable, the lighter the screen is, the better. Like *fusuma*, it is made of a thin wooden grid frame covered on both sides with paper or cloth. A kind of paper honeycomb also makes a good frame. Fairly thin, long hinges are used at the joints of the panels, which are then covered with cloth or paper. A border is placed only on the outer perimeter of the whole screen, not around each separate panel. As mentioned earlier, *sudare* or *yoshizu* screens may be placed in an upright frame to make a gorgeous folding screen. Shoji may also be used with pleasing results.

Folding screens covered with gold or silver paper are put out on auspicious occasions in Japan. These are placed behind the main guest, or at weddings, behind the bride and groom. They may be used in a similar fashion as a striking backdrop for displays, such as the annual Dolls' Festival display in March, or for flower arrangements.

SINGLE-LEAF SCREENS. Another kind of independently standing partition-screen is the *tsuitate*. It is a screen with only one panel with two supporting legs, one on each side. Unlike the folding screen, which consists of several panels linked together, the single-leaf screen is not especially large. It is often placed in the formal entranceway to prevent the interior of the house from being open to view. In restaurants, they are often used to partition off space for different groups of guests.

Its range of possible uses today makes the single-leaf screen very convenient. It would be useful, for example, if one should decide to turn part of the living room into a small bar, or perhaps in partitioning off the living room from the dining area. By laying a few tatami in an area separated by one or more of these screens, one can make a simple impromptu Japanese corner which could then be utilized for entertaining or studying Japanese flower arrangement or tea ceremony. The charm of all this is that the creation of such a setting is achieved by simply putting a screen and tatami in the desired spot.

FOLDING SCREENS

The use of hinges permits folding screens to stand independently in a V or W shape.

VARIATIONS

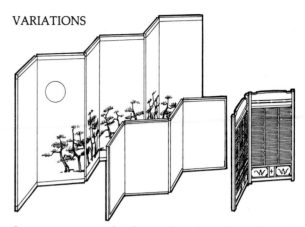

Screens may vary in height, number of panels, and kind of material used.

Folding screen used for the tea ceremony.

SINGLE-LEAF SCREEN VARIATIONS

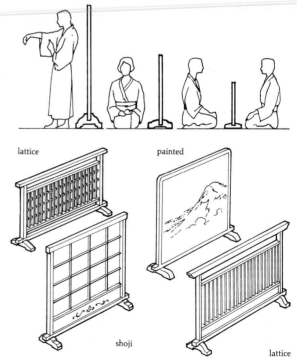

lattice   painted

shoji   lattice

THE ALCOVE

A favorite painting, a handful of flowers, or a rustic vase exquisitely framed in the alcove—understatement is the key to decoration in the Japanese home.

83. An alcove in the entranceway.

84. A tiny alcove near a staircase.

85. A corner converted into an alcove.

86. An ingeniously simple alcove.

87. A base of beautifully grained wood.

88. A shoji window provides illumination for the alcove.

89. A wood and lacquer alcove.

90. A pastel color scheme is most effective.

91. A tatami alcove.

CROSS SECTION

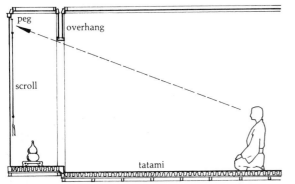

An overhang conceals the peg and the thick threads by which scrolls are hung.

CROSS SECTION OF BASE

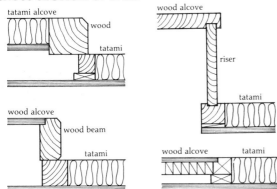

Different materials are possible, but tatami and wood are most commonly used. The wood edging is from 4–6 in. in height and may be raised another 8–12 in.

A hanging alcove.

THE ALCOVE

The development of the Japanese alcove (*tokonoma*) was influenced by a change in art connoisseurship several hundred years ago. In the Kamakura (1185–1392) and Muromachi (1392–1568) periods, a large number of Chinese paintings and art objects were imported into Japan and became the primary focus of attention. Among these imported art works, the hanging scroll figured particularly prominently. It became customary to hang this on the wall, with a low table placed before it furnished with such articles as a candlestand, a censer, or a vase. What was at first a movable display space gradually came to be an immovable fixture, staggered shelves (see opposite page) were added, and the alcove became a part of the interior plan. It is found today in the drawing room or tea ceremony room in homes, and in Japanese-style rooms in hotels.

Construction of the Base
Since it was originally designed as a display dais, the base of the alcove is generally raised slightly. There are many ways of doing this. The most commonly used method these days is to use a wooden beam about 4–6 inches high, either rounded or square, to mark the division between the alcove and the floor of the room, and then to make the alcove floor of wood or tatami the same height. Formerly, it was common to raise it higher than this, by inserting a riser under the beam to increase the height up to 8–12 inches.

Another method is to make the alcove the same level as the floor of the room (see Pl. 86). In this case it is necessary to distinguish this from the rest of the room by using a different kind of material, whereas the base of the raised alcove described above can be made of the same material. To build this kind of floor-level alcove in a carpeted room, for example, one can make an area of wooden flooring, 12–20 inches in width, along one side of a room. The existing wall space can be used for a hanging display, and the wooden area for exhibiting flower arrangements.

A simpler form is the hanging alcove. (See bottom photo on this page.) This is particularly suitable for relatively small rooms. Since the platform is suspended from the ceiling, it allows room for an ordinary floor beneath it.

Another simple idea is to install a thick wooden platform against a wall without the beam placed between the platform and the rest of the floor as described earlier. In this case, however, as well as that of the hanging alcove, not only the surface but also the edge of the platform is visible. Thus the use of good-quality, thick wood, or wood with a lacquer finish, is recommended.

One can also install a platform like this made not of wood but of tatami, which has the effect of making a room, especially a carpeted room, seem all the more Japanese. By placing the tatami in a wooden frame fitted with casters, one has a movable piece of furnishing which can also be used as a bench, a desk, or a table.

It will be recalled that the alcove was originally a plain or lacquered wood table, on top of which ornaments were arranged, with a picture on the wall behind. If this kind of alcove is preferred, it is important that the table be low and that the arrangement of objects be simple. The effect is even better if a few Japanese-style cushions are placed in front of the table.

The Alcove Pillar

One side of the alcove forms a corner with the adjacent wall, but the other extends midway into the room itself, and is supported by a pillar. Since this pillar is conspicuous, it is necessary to use attractive, rounded wood for it. Right up until the end of the Edo period (1615–1868) the building of an alcove was the privilege of only the samurai and selected merchants; thus, like the gateway and the formal entranceway, it came to be a status symbol. Since the Japanese ideal of beauty accorded great importance to the preservation and use of the unspoiled essence of beauty, carved wood was avoided, and only the very rarest wood—flawless or sometimes left unstripped, and absolutely straight—was sought after and prized. In accordance, the background of the alcove should be simply designed to enhance the beauty of this pillar, as well as the scroll and other articles on display.

Lighting and Decoration

To provide illumination for the alcove, a shoji window can be built into the side of the alcove itself, or light from other sources can be used. In the past, a candlestand served as both illumination and decoration. However, as the development of paper shoji made rooms brighter in general, the custom of using a candlestand fell into disuse. These days, of course, electric lighting can be employed instead of shoji lighting. An overhead light or spotlight can be fixed onto the back of the overhang; if not, it can be sunk into the ceiling. In addition, a paper-covered lamp can be placed on the floor of the alcove.

The articles displayed in the alcove should vary according to the season, the guest, or the occasion. Although one may devote much attention to acquiring suitable pieces, they are never put out all at once, as is also true of the formal entranceway. Rather, the host tries to create different settings and offer fresh topics of conversation while bearing in mind, for example, a guest's fondness for a certain kind of flower or interest in a particular kind of pottery. In this way, the alcove can be seen as bringing together not only people but also art and life in one's own home.

Relationship with the Garden

The relationship between the room in which the alcove is located, and the garden, if there is one, is another point which should not be neglected. It is customary for the visitor, having once admired the objects on display, to sit in the position from which he can appreciate the south- or east-facing garden. It may seem strange to have the objects on display behind one's back, but the idea of sitting closest to the alcove requires that no other person be between the main guest and it, in order that the guest may appreciate it fully. In addition, since the entrance to the room in this kind of arrangement is on the southern or eastern side, the guest is farthest away from the area where people will be coming and going.

ALCOVE VARIATIONS

STAGGERED SHELF VARIATIONS

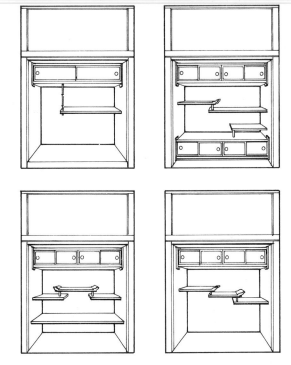

THE ROOM FOR THE TEA CEREMONY

A corner, a room, a cottage—all may offer a temporary haven where one shares the warmth of friends or finds comfort and peace in solitude.

92. Guests wait here to be called by the host of the tea ceremony.

93. The bound stone symbolizes entry into a different world.

94. The entrance is purposefully narrow.

95. Natural materials alone are used.

96. Natural-colored clay is preferred for the walls.

97. The ideal tea room is surrounded by nature.

98. Simple lines and intricate patterns coexist harmoniously.

99. Natural lighting is the only source of illumination.

Host and guests at a tea ceremony.

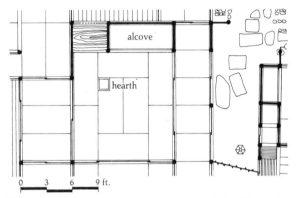

Plan of eight-tatami mat tea room of the Urasenke Foundation.

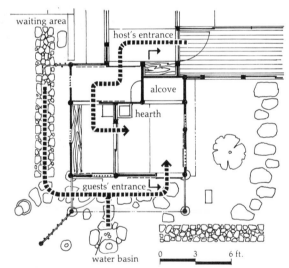

Plan of Tai-an, a two-tatami mat tea room.

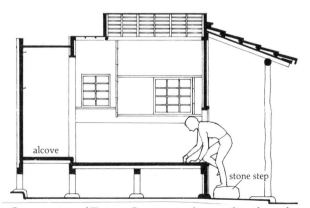

Cross section of Tai-an. Guests enter by crawling through a narrow, low entrance.

THE ROOM FOR THE TEA CEREMONY

What is the tea ceremony? Simply put, it is a gathering of a few people to share a bowl of tea. The tea used is in powder form and is a vibrant green color. It is whisked until slightly frothy and served hot in a tea bowl about the size of a soup bowl. Sugar and cream are never added, but to make the astringent taste of the tea more palatable, traditional Japanese sweet cakes are provided before the tea is served.

The aesthetic consciousness underlying the present-day tea ceremony wherein everything—the utensils for making the tea, the drinking bowls, the arrangement of the alcove, the sequence of movements, etc.—coalesces into a unity of object, person, and space, came to be established between the end of the fifteenth century and the end of the sixteenth. Today, tea ceremony teachers in Japan, the U.S., and elsewhere give training in what is considered one of the polite arts of Japan to a large number of students. The etiquette of the tea ceremony is so complex and refined, however, that this formidable code has come to have little or no meaning to many Japanese. If one can develop a genuine liking for powdered tea, then an interest in the forms and in the quality of the tea bowls and other utensils will follow naturally, and one can refer to a number of books available in English.

Design

The tea room (*chashitsu*), whether it be somewhere in the house itself, or a detached building, is a place where one should feel as though one is in a completely different world. Two things which symbolize this separation from the world are the *kekkai*, a small stone bound with rope, and the tiny entrance. As the guest approaches the tea room from the garden, placement of the *kekkai* in the middle of the pathway tells him whether another tea ceremony is in progress, and whether he should wait in a specially built shelter. The *kekkai* marks the boundary between the everyday world and the non-everyday world, as well as the boundary of privacy where the voices of people in the tea room cannot be heard.

The *nijiriguchi* through which guests enter is approximately 28 inches high and 24 inches wide, and guests must enter on their knees. This tiny entrance was and still is the symbol of equality and peace. In the past, even lords had to prostrate themselves, a symbol of respect, to enter the tea room, and samurai had to leave their swords, a symbol of power, outside. Today, even distinguished guests must literally crawl through the entrance, and, instead of the sword, pretension and status are discarded upon entering the tea room.

Once one has entered the tea ceremony room, however, the small entrance no longer seems to be particularly small for, since the dimensions of the materials used—such as the size of the shoji and the squares of paper within them—are on a slightly reduced scale, the room appears bigger than it really is. Nevertheless, the standard size is only 4½ tatami mats, about 9 feet by 9 feet. Even smaller ones of two mats, approximately 6 feet by 6 feet, can be found. There is also an alcove, the size of one tatami mat, 3 feet by 6 feet, or less. The ceiling has an average height of 6¼ feet and slopes upward to about 7¼ feet at its highest point.

Japanese architecture is in general very simple, but there is a dense complexity of design in the tea room. Within a very limited space is a richness of variety in details. Utilized nevertheless with the utmost simplicity, this approach—known as the "hermitage" or "mountain retreat in the middle of the city" way of thinking—is an attempt to create a natural setting in the midst of the ostentatiousness of city life. The use of such a wide variety of materials in such a confined area reflects a desire to get the best out of a bare minimum. The few links with the outside world are the separate entrances for the host and guests, the translucent shoji windows, and, occasionally, a window in the ceiling. This feeling of intimacy creates a special atmosphere and the perfect mood for contemplation and relaxation.

Two tatami mats are virtually the minimum for a tea room, but other designs are possible as well. The location of the host's seat depends on where the hearth is situated, while the guest should sit in front of the alcove. The hearth is an important requisite for performing the tea ceremony, but it is not absolutely necessary to have one built into the floor. Instead, a brazier shaped like a shallow box is quite adequate, or one could purchase an electric brazier, or even bring hot water in a thermos from the kitchen. This depends, however, on how far one has mastered the art of the tea ceremony. To a connoisseur, a hearth is absolutely necessary, even if only as a formality.

A Separate World, A Spiritual Shelter

Should one want to make an orthodox tea room, it would be best to refer to a specialized book on the subject for full details. But it may be more meaningful, especially if one is not particularly interested in the tea ceremony, to reconsider the philosophy of the tea room. After all, the physical setting for the partaking of the green tea was designed to be like a tiny cosmos, separated from the daily world, where the mind could become clear, and the harmony between people restored. For people of today as well, with their hectic lifestyles, this kind of spiritual shelter has much to offer. The actual place can be a second home, a cottage next to the house, or simply a room in the house itself. For Americans, a Japanese-style room is already a setting which is removed from their everyday experience. Thus it is not necessary to reproduce a tea ceremony room meticulously.

Above all, it is a question of being able, in the midst of our modern urban existence, to achieve peace of mind by sitting quietly in a tiny room. The need to occasionally retreat even from one's own family might also unintentionally motivate the spirit of today's tea ceremony.

For those who wish to think along more sociable lines, it would be possible to build a tea pavilion outside for garden parties. In this case, it would be better, rather than preserving the closed-in feeling of an orthodox tea room, to use regular-sized shoji and add a veranda to make a more open structure. In the home itself, a small room adjacent to the living room could be used as a tea room for special occasions, and as a recreation or guest room at other times.

CEILING DESIGNS

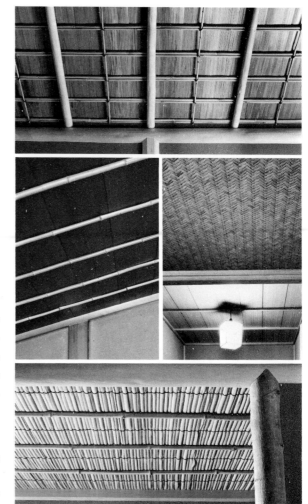

The use of different materials in their natural form produces striking patterns.

WINDOW PATTERNS

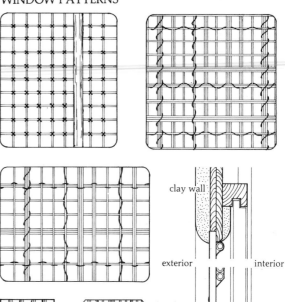

clay wall

exterior   interior

bamboo
lattice

                            shoji

twine

DETAIL

THE JAPANESE WAY OF SITTING

Grounded and secure, one's line of vision and outlook are startlingly altered.

101. A portable hearth on tatami.

100. A table and legless chairs.

102. A sunken table and benches.

103. A combination table and hearth.

104. A sunken hearth in a country-style setting.

105. A sunken hearth in a mountain retreat.

106. A low table with heating element underneath.

107. Traditional plan with tatami and low table.

formal   informal (men)   informal (women)

FURNITURE

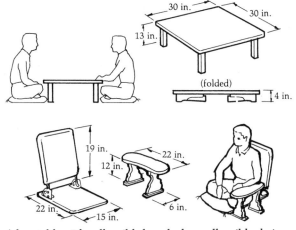

A low table with collapsible legs, legless collapsible chairs, and independently standing armrests can be easily moved around and stored away.

HEARTH AND BRAZIER ARRANGEMENTS

A free-standing heat source provides 360 degrees of warmth.

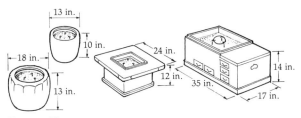

Types of braziers.

THE JAPANESE WAY OF SITTING

The Japanese custom of sitting on the floor instead of on chairs is closely related to the habit of removing one's shoes before entering the house. In the past in a country where it rains an average of 120 days a year, simple dirt-floored rooms would become very damp. Thus floors came to be laid with planks or bamboo raised 1–1½ feet above ground level, and straw or matting was spread on them for people to sit on. Eventually, as we have seen, tatami came to be used to cover the entire floor. The custom of removing one's shoes still continues today in Japan even in Western-style homes.

Of course, sitting on the floor is not a particularly Japanese custom. It is practiced by many people all over the world, and is quite common on carpeted floors. Furthermore, as the Japanese way of life becomes more and more Westernized, the Western way of sitting on chairs, especially at mealtime or when entertaining guests, has become popular. The wearing of trousers instead of kimono also has the effect of making the knees visible, and destroys the visual poise and balance of the traditional Japanese sitting posture.

Despite these trends, however, taking one's shoes off and sitting on the floor—regardless of whether it is tatami, carpeting, or just wood—still instills in the Japanese a feeling of relaxation. And, as long as some vestiges of the traditional sitting posture remain, the traditionally low perspective or line of sight will continue to influence ways of looking at objects, nature, and even people.

Sitting around the Hearth

Before the idea of the chimney was developed in Japan, houses used to have a hearth cut into the floor, and smoke would escape through a window high up on the wall or in the roof. This method is of course no longer appropriate to current living arrangements, but the idea of having a center around which people can sit is appealing. Recently, the popularity of this kind of old-fashioned hearth, the *irori*, has grown among urban dwellers in Japan.

The most important point to keep in mind is the central position of the hearth. Unlike Western schemes where the fireplace is built against a wall, a Japanese-style hearth built or placed in the middle of a room allows a 360-degree area of heating. Moreover, because little or no furniture is used, proximity to the heat source is increased, as well as the sense of intimacy of a gathering.

When installing a hearth in the home, it is important to provide adequate ventilation by placing a hood over the hearth and putting an exhaust duct in the ceiling. The bottom of the hearth should be about 4–12 inches below floor level, and lined with iron or copper sheeting, on top of which ashes or sand should be spread. Incidentally, the Japanese hearth does not normally have a blazing fire as is the case with its Western counterpart. Coals are brought in from outside to provide enough heat to keep a kettle of water hot or to cook a pot of stew, either placed on the fire or suspended by an adjustable hook.

Instead of a hearth, a low table can be used to provide a room with a center. Though an old-fashioned Japanese brazier can still be used as a portable heater, it can also serve as the base of an attractive glass-top coffee table. Whatever the arrangement, cushions placed around the hearth, table, or brazier, will provide comfort as well as a bit of color to the room.

Another possibility is to hollow out part of the center of a table and build a small-scale hearth there. Good for use as a kind of barbecue, where food can be cooked and eaten on the spot, or sake warmed, this method is often used in Japanese country-style restaurants. Dishes such as sukiyaki or *nabemono*, a kind of fondue, are cooked on a gas ring or a hot plate either placed on the table top or else fitted into the table itself. In the rainy climate of Japan, outdoor barbecues are not a very practical idea, so they are brought indoors instead.

Today, one of the most popular household items in Japan is the *kotatsu*, a low table with an infrared lamp, equipped with a thermostat and a protective mesh, attached to the underside of the table. A cover is usually placed over the table, and another table-like surface is put on top of that. This keeps the heat in under the table, and improves its heating efficiency. Although very simple to use, the *kotatsu* can, however, be uncomfortable as there is little room for one's legs underneath.

As a result, many people have taken to sinking one part of the floor below the level of the rest and sitting with their feet resting in the resulting hollow, called a *horigotatsu*. A permanent fixture is created but the table may be removed, and the hole covered, when they are not needed, and the room may be used for other purposes. In a room with tatami, a half-size tatami (3 feet by 3 feet) or a wooden board can be used as a cover, and also provide a kind of display area (see Pl. 54 and title page). When floor heating is used, it is a good idea to heat both the floor of the sunken area and the floor where people sit. For this, one can use either hot water piping laid under the floor, or an electric mat.

Some Words of Caution

For the unaccustomed, sitting on the floor can be unpleasant and even painful. In particular, the formal sitting posture is difficult for today's young Japanese to maintain for long periods, though in fact the informal posture is all that is required in most situations. Cushions can make sitting on the floor more comfortable, as can the use of a small, legless chair. Separate, independently standing armrests also offer some support.

If your feet should fall asleep while you are sitting on the floor, do not attempt to stand up right away. Extend your legs and massage them gently, and try to stand up only after the prickly feeling is gone. If you know in advance that you will be sitting Japanese-style, wear comfortable, loose-fitting clothes. Jeans, for example, will constrict the flow of blood to the lower torso and create discomfort and pain. It is also a good idea to check if your socks have any holes in them before you leave home, rather than discover this after arriving at your destination! Some people even carry an extra pair of clean socks to change into, especially when they know there is going to be a tatami floor.

KOTATSU

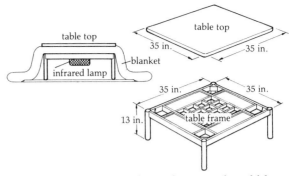

The table top is covered with wood on one side and felt on the other, ideal for playing mahjong or cards. In the summertime, the infrared lamp can be removed.

A fully assembled *kotatsu*.

SUNKEN *KOTATSU*

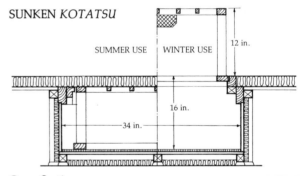

Cross Section

In the summertime, the table frame is stored in a floor cavity and covered either with a piece of tatami or wood.

(Designed by J. Yoshimura)

LIGHTING TECHNIQUES

Soft, soothing, and beautiful, Japanese lighting techniques will heighten your appreciation of the world around you.

108. Light sources are traditionally placed low.

109. Soft, filtered lighting is best.

110. Harsh illumination is avoided.

111. The natural reflecting quality of shoji is inimitable.

112. Design is never divorced from function.

113. Lampshade made from one sheet of paper.

114. Lampshade with script.

115. Lamp with fiberglass shade.

116. Paper lampshade with bamboo ribs.

117. Wall light fixture.

118. Ceiling light fixture.

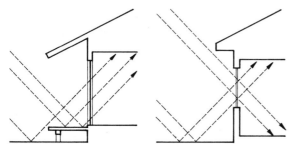

Reflection of light in a Japanese house (left) and a Western house (right).

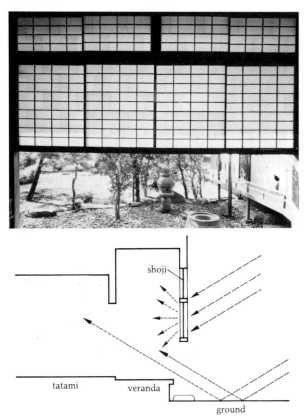

Reflection of light in Koho-an Tea Room.

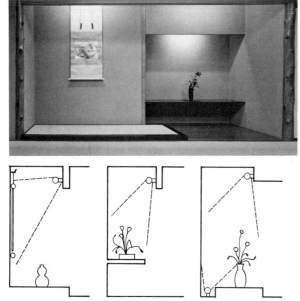

Lighting techniques for the alcove.

LIGHTING TECHNIQUES

In the traditional Japanese house with its low, overhanging eaves, the lower parts of a room receive the most light while the higher areas become progressively darker. This is because sunlight, blocked as it is by the eaves, enters the room after being reflected off the ground or off the veranda, and travels in an upward direction. Light becomes less bright the farther it goes, which in this case means the higher it goes. The Western window, on the other hand, admits sunlight directly—a curtain being used to block it out when necessary—and the rays of light travel in a downward direction.

In Japan, lighting devices for the home originally used to be placed on the floor because of the way light entered it, as described above. It is the same with garden illumination: instead of hanging lights from trees, the Japanese used stone lanterns, placed on the ground. This kind of lighting is, moreover, especially suited to the custom of sitting on the floor, discussed earlier. Since tables and other surfaces which require illumination were low, lamps situated on the floor were ideal.

The development of glass in Japan came very late; thus the technique of using glass to provide direct, bright illumination, and to reflect light in a sparkling, glittering way, did not flourish. Rather, the soft illumination which enters a room through the white paper of the shoji can be said to be the basic characteristic of Japanese-style lighting, and indirect lighting is vastly preferred to harsh, direct lighting.

If modern illumination can be compared with the brilliant sun, perhaps traditional Japanese illumination may be said to represent the luminous moon. Part of the tranquil beauty of the traditional Japanese home is captured through the use of indirect lighting, which, in addition, complements the soft textures and natural colors of a room with tatami and shoji. Today, in Japan, however, the sense of enjoyment associated with the play of light and shadows seems to have been forgotten, and the concept of creating atmosphere through the use of natural or indirect lighting, such as that used in a tea room, has almost disappeared. Although bright lighting can be used attractively, soft lighting can add a new dimension to the home. Here are some ideas.

Shoji
We have already seen how shoji can serve as a room partition. It can also serve as a kind of wall illumination. Depending on light conditions, shoji can reflect light to make a room brighter or be used to produce a beautiful silhouette effect when shadows are created by the lattice frame of the shoji or trees outside.

As has been mentioned already, the shoji can be suspended as a partition-wall, with a spotlight shining on it from behind. 8mm films or slides can be projected onto the side without the wooden frame. When not required, the shoji can be hung on the wall out of the way, or in front of a window instead of a curtain.

Another idea is to fix a light bulb onto a wall and then put a small shoji-like panel in front of it, or, something like a Japanese kite can also be interesting. If a kite is used, the lighting efficiency can be improved by inclining it slightly, either upwards or downwards. This can be easily mounted and held in place with thick wire.

Andon/Chochin

The *andon* is usually placed on the floor, though it can also be stood on a desk or a shelf. The basic pattern is to have a hollow, upright wooden frame around the sides of which a shade made of shoji paper is affixed, leaving the ends open to allow heat to escape. This is then mounted on a stand. (See Pl. 114.)

Although the *andon* could be moved from room to room indoors, it was not intended for use as a kind of torch to be carried around all the time. When going outdoors, the Japanese used a *chochin*, a portable lantern made of thin bamboo cane wound into a spiral, to the outside of which paper was glued. (See p. 80.) As it could be folded flat, it was easily portable. Later, *chochin* came to be hung on shop fronts, bearing the symbol or name of the shop, and thus can be seen as one of the first forms of suspended lighting in Japan. Although the use of *andon* has sadly become only a novelty, *chochin* still thrive, especially in the entertainment districts of cities, and one can see large red *chochin* outside places serving Japanese food.

Chochin are ideal for use at garden parties. Both the *chochin* and the electric cord can be suspended in a line, from a wire running from one tree to the next. Or instead of electricity, candles can be used, as was the case with the original *chochin*. *Chochin* can also be hung as illumination from the eaves of a veranda.

Ceiling and Wall Lighting

As was said earlier, originally the custom of putting light fixtures on indoor ceilings and walls hardly existed at all in Japan. So it came to be that, when such fixtures were eventually adopted, the *chochin*, which had been used mainly outdoors, the *andon*, and various devices based on the shape and techniques of shoji, were adapted for this purpose.

The *chochin* is particularly effective in giving a Japanese touch to a room when suspended from the ceiling. Hanging an *andon* from the ceiling is also possible. Usually the bottom of the *andon* shade is left open, but if it is hung from the ceiling it should be closed or else left with only a small opening. If one should use shoji, it is best to suspend it using a hook from which it can be easily removed, since dust will collect on it.

The points to pay attention to are more or less the same when the lighting is fixed to the wall. A simple bracket extending from the wall can be used.

In either case, the use of paper poses a fire risk; particularly if there are children around, a floor lamp can be easily overturned. Fortunately, white non-flammable plastic sheeting looks very much like real shoji paper and can be used as a substitute.

This kind of plastic sheeting can be used effectively to provide illumination for large areas such as the ceiling in the kitchen or the floor of a living room. The use of reed panels or even mesh to diffuse light is another way of providing indirect lighting for the home.

Instructions for making a Japanese-style lamp may be found in the do-it-yourself section in the back of this book.

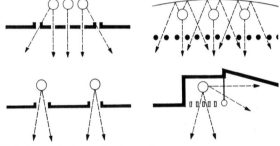

Lighting techniques for the ceiling.

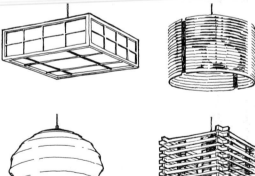

Lampshade variations.

THE BATH

A time and place to cleanse the body and to refresh the soul.

119. A wood tub with matching accessories.

120. A bath with a garden view.

121. A bath in the mountains.

THE BATH

The Japanese bath (*furo*) is designed to be used by more than one person at a time. It is deep enough for the water to cover the shoulders of a seated person, so that if one sits with knees tucked up, two or more people may sit together. One is expected to scrub down and rinse oneself off *outside* the bathtub before getting into it for the tub is simply for warming and relaxing the body. In Japan, small children often enter the tub with their mother or father. Then, it is not simply a matter of taking a bath to clean oneself, but is also an opportunity to talk about all that has happened during the day. Another pleasant custom is for people to wash each other's backs before soaking together.

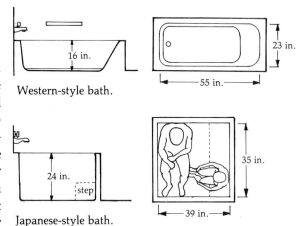

Western-style bath.

Japanese-style bath.

Layout, Materials, and Setting

First of all, the area used for washing one's body is outside the bathtub. It usually has a shower attachment high up on the wall, and hot and cold water taps lower down. A place for the water to drain away is of course also necessary.

The shower attachment should be flexible enough so that it can be used by a person either standing or sitting on a small stool. To wash oneself, one takes water from the bathtub in a small pail, but a shower attachment alone will suffice.

Some bathtubs are fairly small, but a length of at least four feet is desirable, since this is roughly the length taken up by an adult sitting with legs outstretched. As for width, one person requires about 32–36 inches. The tub should be deep enough for the water to cover the shoulders of a seated adult. However, if a bathtub of this depth is simply placed on the floor of the bathroom, getting into it becomes a hazardous business. It is usually, therefore, sunk a little into the floor. When this is not possible, a step or ledge can be built inside or outside the bathtub.

Another characteristic of the Japanese bath is that the water is not changed after each person is done. Since it is used only for drawing water and soaking, the same water can be shared by everyone. A wood or plastic cover is placed over the tub when it is not being used to keep the water warm and to reduce the amount of water vapor. The water can also be reheated as necessary. The usual method is for the water to be taken out through a pipe in the bottom of the bathtub and heated in a small boiler, before being fed back into the tub.

Wood, especially Japanese cypress with its marvelous fragrance, is the best material for a tub, but recently fiberglass-reinforced plastic and stainless steel tubs have become popular. Wood may be used for the removable slatted platform placed on the floor of the washing area, and for the walls. The use of rock or stone for the tub and the walls creates the atmosphere of a natural hot spring. Since the bath is a place for relaxation, it is a good idea to design it in such a way to give one the impression of bathing in natural surroundings.

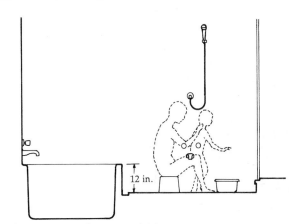

Cross section of Japanese bath.

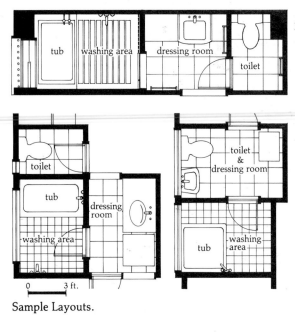

Sample Layouts.

Accessories

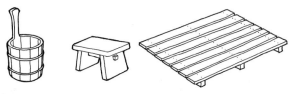

hand bucket   stool   slatted platform

73

MATERIALS REQUIRED FOR 2 FT. × 2 FT. SHOJI:
Wood for crosspieces: 1 in. × 1 in. × 2 ft. (4)
Wood for interior: ¾ in. × ¾ in. × 2 ft. (6)
Paper
Glue
Nails
Hooked nails: 2 in. (4)
TOOLS REQUIRED:
Saw, chisel, hammer, plane, sandpaper

PROJECT 1:
Hanging Shoji (*Kakeshoji*)

Ordinary shoji are designed to be used as sliding doors, and runners must be made for the top and bottom. A considerable amount of skill and effort are required to hollow out these runners accurately, and once in position the shoji have a permanent location even though they may be removed temporarily. Hanging shoji, on the other hand, are portable and may be hung anywhere. They are often found in tea ceremony rooms and rooms with a Japanese-style alcove.

A soft wood that has been well dried to prevent warping is best. Extremely narrow slats of wood are preferred, but slightly thicker slats are easier to work with and may be used instead. Simplified methods of joinery will be explained here.

Making such small pieces is intricate work in itself, but even more difficult is to then put together a lattice. For this, an electric saw with a guard will be necessary. The size of the shoji should be tailored so that the window frame, if there is one, is concealed. The upper crosspiece should extend beyond the edge of the frame by 1½ times its width to enable it to be supported by nails inserted into the wall. The side supports should also extend beneath the bottom of the frame to prevent it from leaning to one side by 1½ times their own width.

Hooked nails from which to hang the shoji are nailed at the four corners (Fig. 1–B). If there is no place to insert nails into the wall around the window, transparent thread hung from the ceiling may be used to suspend the shoji (Fig. 5–B).

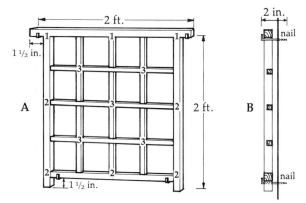

1.(A) Three types of joints are used in making a shoji frame: 1) A-type joints between the upper crosspieces and supports, and between the upper crosspieces and lattice; 2) B-type joints between the lower crosspieces and supports, and between the lower crosspieces and lattice; and 3) C-type joints between lattice slats.
(B) Hooked nails are used to hang the shoji from the frame.

Joinery
Broadly speaking, there are three types of joints used in this kind of carpentry. A-type joints are those between the upper crosspieces and supports, and those between the upper crosspieces and lattice (Fig. 1–A). Since the top of the crosspiece is usually not visible, it makes no difference if the supports and the ends of the lattice extend above the top of the frame, and the joints can be simplified as shown in Fig. 2–A1. Glue and nails are used for the joints, and since paper is affixed to the frame, nail heads are neatly concealed.

B-type joints are those between the lower crosspiece and supports, and those between the lower crosspiece and the lattice (Fig. 1–A). Since, in this case, the edges and lower half of the frame are clearly visible, care should be taken that the edges of the lattice are neatly finished (Fig. 2–B). The joints should only penetrate about ⅔ of the total width of the crosspiece and be finished off with glue and nails. Again, nail heads can be neatly concealed with paper.

B-type joints necessitate use of such tools as a chisel and are thus more complicated than A-type joints. To simplify construction, A-type joints may be used (Fig. 2–B1), though in such cases, in order to conceal the edges of the lattice frame, paper should be fixed to the edges of the frame and then cut.

C-type joints are used between lattice slats (Fig 1–A). The lattice should ideally be chamfered, so that the point where slats intersect should appear as in Fig. 2–C. The cross section should

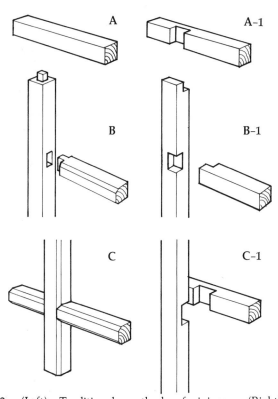

2. (Left) Traditional method of joinery. (Right) Simplified method of joinery.

measure $5/16$–$10/16$ inch, but since this is extremely difficult to achieve, this design can be simplified to something along the lines of Fig. 2–C1.

When one has completed construction of the frame and lattice, and just about assembled it, minute adjustments can then be applied to those parts that will be hidden by the paper, and sections planed and sandpapered.

Applying the Paper

Japanese shoji paper is the best material, but thin art paper or tracing paper may be used. To prevent the paper from becoming loose later, a little moisture should be sprayed on it to make it expand before it is put onto the frame. But if the paper is put on too tightly, the frame which the paper is attached to is liable to bend and warp.

The paper strips are pasted from left to right on the outside starting from the bottom (Fig. 3–A1), to keep dust from entering if the paper becomes loose. The paper is generally cut just in from the edge of the back of the frame (Fig. 3–A) or partially wound around corners (Fig. 3–B). In highly crafted work, the edge of the frame can be beveled so as to enable the paper to lie flush with the frame (Fig. 3–C), but such superior craftsmanship is at a premium today, even in Japan. Funorin glue is the best adhesive to use since the consistency is readily adjusted by the addition of hot water. Polyvinyl glue, ordinary laundry starch, or wallpaper paste is also suitable. Care should be taken that the adhesive used is not of the fast-setting variety because this will make application of the paper difficult. With funorin, the rate at which the paper is stretched over the frame while it is becoming dry matches the rate at which the glue sets, and the danger of overstretching is thus minimized.

It is best to try the glue out first on a spare piece of paper to make sure that it does not affect the color of the paper and that it is easily removable. The paste should be applied to the frame and not to the paper.

Shade Variations

The beauty of shoji is due in part to the myriad designs possible (Fig. 4). When designing the frame and lattice interior, one may wish to experiment with just horizontal supports or just vertical supports or even with just the outside frame. The size of the lattice sections, especially when paper is used, helps to make the size of a room seem larger or smaller.

Hanging Shoji Used Elsewhere

Shoji can be further employed as a means of partitioning or even as a kind of lampshade. As mentioned in the chapter on shoji, one can suspend a large shoji between two rooms, such as the dining and living rooms, and use it as a room divider and as an interesting illuminating device. If a shoji is placed at an oblique angle in the corner of a room (Fig. 5–A) and some kind of illumination placed behind it (Fig. 5–A), it not only serves as a kind of corner illumination but can also be used to create a variety of effects.

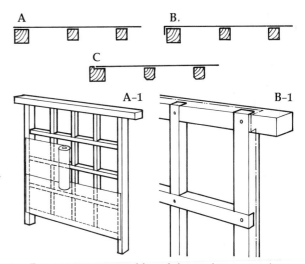

3. Paper strips are pasted from left to right, starting from the bottom. The paper may be cut in from the edge of the frame (A, A–1), partially wound around corners (B, B–1), or lie flush with the frame (C).

4. Patterns for frame and interior.

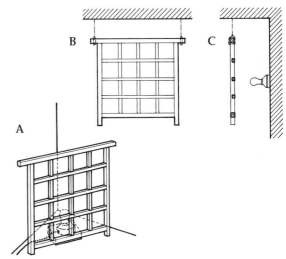

5. Hanging shoji may be used to cover a window or to provide a form of corner illumination.

Wood for main frame pieces:
 ½ in. × ½ in. × 12 in. (8)
 1 ½ in. × 1 ½ in. × 8 in. (4)
Wood for interior pieces: ¼ in. × ¼ in. × 12 in. (4)
 ¼ in. × ¼ in. × 8 in. (8)
Wood for top of frame: 1 in. × ¼ in. × 12 in.
Paper
Glue
TOOLS REQUIRED:
 Saw, plane, sandpaper

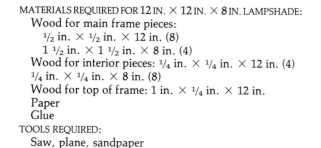

1.　(Left) Ceiling light fixture. (Right) Wall light fixture.

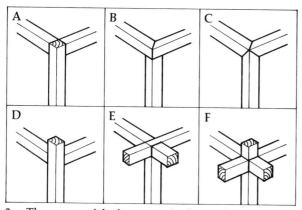

2.　The corners of the frame may be designed so that none or only some of the struts protrude.

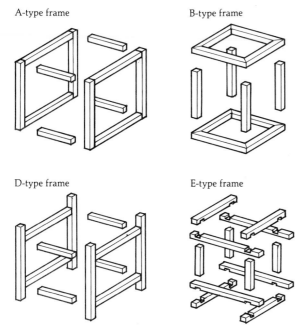

3.　Typse of frame construction.

PROJECT 2:
Shoji Lampshade

In addition to its partitioning function, shoji also serve as a kind of illuminating device. Here we shall consider use of a light fixture either suspended from the ceiling or bracketed to the wall. Construction of a shade for both of these is the same. Both the top and bottom of the cube are left open. For the suspended light, the four sides are designed to produce a shoji-type effect (Fig. 1–A), whereas in the bracketed version only three are thus designed, the fourth being used to bracket the device to the wall (Fig. 1–B). These may all be considered as mini-shoji. Construction of the basic lattice frame is explained in Project 1.

Construction of the Frame
Since the frame is square, problems may arise over construction of the corners. It can either be designed, as in Fig. 2, where none of the struts protrude (A, B, C), or where some are made to protrude (D, E, F). A-, B-, D-, and E-type designs are not so difficult, but a C-type calls for considerable skill and patience, and an F-type is the most difficult design.

Let us first consider the simplest method—those joints that can be glued together. To build an A-type frame, the intervening struts are inserted only after the top and bottom of the frame have been glued together (Fig. 3–A). In a B-type frame, the top and bottom of the frame are constructed of sections that have been sawn off at 45 degrees (Fig. 2–B), and when inserted in place, should create a solid joint (Fig. 3–B). A C-type design is a more complicated three-dimensional version of this B-type design. A D-type frame is similar to an A-type, except that one of the intervening struts is allowed to protrude above the top of the frame. An E-type frame is created by constructing the top and bottom of the frame using joints as shown in Fig. 2–E, and then inserting the intervening struts (Fig. 3–E).

Accurate construction of an F-type frame is like a puzzle for those who wish to try it. It is simpler to attach short pieces of wood to the top and bottom of an E-type design to produce the same effect. Having completed two sides of either an E- or F-type frame, care should be taken when inserting the intervening struts that right angles are preserved in all three dimensions.

The lattice should be designed one side at a time (Fig. 4), fitted into the frame, and then glued.

How to Erect the Completed Product
When the shade is designed for hanging from the ceiling, a small lattice (Fig. 5–A) or a single slat of wood (Fig. 5–B) should be incorporated into the top of the shade. A small groove, just wide enough to accommodate the cord, should be carved into one of the lattice pieces or the single slat. The center of gravity must be taken into account so that the shade does not hang at an angle. A knot should be tied in the cord just below the lattice or slat into which the groove has been carved in order to support the shade (Fig. 5–C). This additional lattice or slat should not merely be glued into position, but held firmly in position by means of a tenon and mortise joint.

Another simple design is shown in Fig. 6–A where transparent threads from which the shade hangs are attached to each of the four corners and then tied to the cord. This method will require either a small screw at each of the four corners (Fig. 6–B) or else small holes just large enough for the thread to pass through to be drilled near each corner (Fig. 6–C).

When the bulb is attached directly to a socket in the ceiling, a small gap should be left between the top of the shade and the ceiling, in order to allow heat from the bulb to escape (Fig. 7–A). A paper-covered lattice should be designed for the bottom to hide the bulb.

If the shade is to be affixed to the wall, the frame should be suspended from a hook (Fig. 7–B). If it is to be placed high up on the wall, then a lattice should also be attached to the bottom. But the top should be left open to allow heat to escape.

Paper or Plastic as a Covering

White paper or plastic is attached to the inside of the four sides of a lampshade suspended from the ceiling, and to three sides of a lampshade fixed to the wall. If the light is particularly high, then the lower side of the shade may be covered. At least one side, preferably the top, is left open, and it is from here that the paper or plastic to be used is inserted. If both upper and lower sides are left uncovered, papering is much easier.

Conversion into a Floor Lamp

Prior to the introduction of the light bulb, the major form of illumination was an oil light placed on the floor. The traditional form was the *andon*, and, as shown in Fig. 8–A, this is easily constructed by inserting a light bulb into a wooden stand and surrounding it with a shoji-type shade. An easy method of installing the shade is by pulling it down from above and then inserting screws from inside which are affixed to the supporting pillars.

A similar method can be used for the circular *andon* (see Pl. 113), but a better effect can be achieved by using plastic instead of paper. The circular rings at the top and bottom are connected by at least four supporting struts, and the plastic sheet affixed to the inside. In order to preserve the shape of the plastic sheet, rings, and struts, liberal use should be made of glue.

Frame Variations

Like the hanging shoji described in Project 1, a shade consisting merely of a wooden frame with no paper affixed can be made. Construction of this kind of shade follows almost the same procedure as described above, so suffice it here merely to describe its design.

As shown in Fig. 8–B, this basically consists of slats of wood piled one on top of each other, and designed into a square, pentagon, hexagon, etc. The slats are held together simply by passing a length of wire down a hole drilled right through the frame from top to bottom at each corner. The whole unit can then be easily suspended by using the end of the wire as a hook.

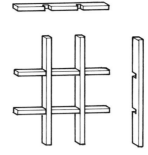

4. The lattice should be designed one side at a time, fitted into the frame, and then glued.

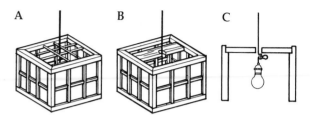

5. Ways to accommodate the cord.

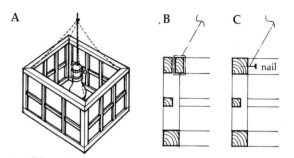

6. Ways of using transparent thread to hang the shade.

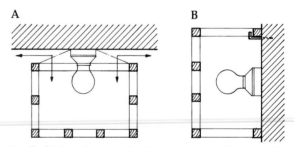

7. (Left) Installation of ceiling fixture. (Right) Installation of wall fixture.

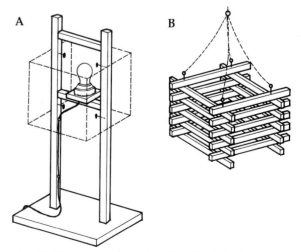

8. (Left) Construction of *andon*. (Right) Shades made without paper.

MATERIALS REQUIRED:
  Socket
  Stem: same diameter as socket, 40 in. long
  Casing pipe
  Cord
  Plug
  Switch
  Planter: 8–10 in. in diameter, 2–3 in. deep
  Cement
  Sand
  Stone aggregate
  Wood:
    1 in. × 2 in. × 12 in. (2)
    ¼ in. × ⅛ in. × 5 in. (1)
  Paper: 15¼ in. × 20 in.
  Wire
TOOLS REQUIRED:
  Saw, screwdriver, cutter, drill

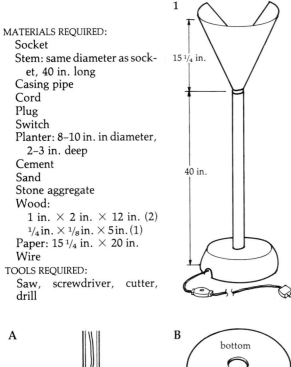

1

15¼ in.

40 in.

A

2 in.

8 in.

B

bottom

2. A small incision must be made in the base of the stem to allow the electric cord to emerge from the bottom. Then a groove must be made at the base of the mold to allow the cord to emerge from the bottom of the base.

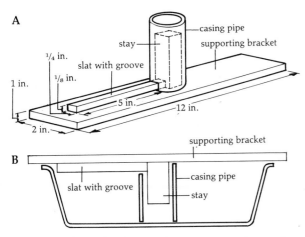

A

casing pipe
stay
supporting bracket
slat with groove
¼ in.
⅛ in.
1 in.
5 in.
12 in.
2 in.

supporting bracket

B

slat with groove
casing pipe
stay

3. A slat of wood with a matching groove, and a wooden stay, are attached to a supporting bracket, and laid across the top of the mold.

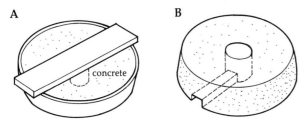

A

concrete

B

4. After pouring in the concrete, the top of the mix must be flattened out. The slat with a groove for the cord and the stay supporting the pipe should come away with the bracket after the concrete has dried. The mold will be ready for removal after a few days, and fine adjustments can then be made.

PROJECT 3:
Floor Lamp with Paper Shade

Described in this section is the type of lamp stand seen in Fig. 1, a unique beauty achieved with using only one sheet of paper for the lampshade.

Roughly speaking, this light consists of a base, supporting stem, electrical fixture, and shade. Since the base is designed to accommodate the supporting stem without falling over, it must be stable. A slab of marble, into which a hole has been sunk, is ideal, but should one be set on designing the base by oneself, concrete is the most suitable material.

The stem may be designed from metal (aluminum or stainless steel), although bamboo creates a much more Japanese mood. It should not be designed as a continuation of the base but should be readily removable, since this makes repairs and changes easy.

The electrical fixture consists of a plug, cord, switch, socket, and bulb. Since the design will depend on the kind of socket available, it is important to buy the socket and decide how it should be affixed before deciding on the size of the stem. The bulb should be from 20–60 watts; anything brighter would be dangerous because the shade is made of paper.

The paper for the shade should be white and translucent. If it is too soft, however, it will not maintain its shape. Ideal for this purpose is shoji paper, 25×38 50 lb. book paper, or a plastic-based type of thick tracing paper.

Construction of the Concrete Base

A base perfect in both size and weight can be designed by pouring concrete into a planter about 8–10 inches in diameter and 2–3 inches deep used as a mold. The casing pipe for the stem should accommodate the stem snugly, though should the pipe prove larger, tape can always be wrapped around the base of the stem to afford a perfect fit. To allow the electric cord to emerge from the bottom of the casing pipe, a small incision should be cut into the base of the pipe (Fig. 2–A). Then, to allow the cord to emerge from the bottom of the base, a groove should be made at the base of the mold (Fig. 2–B). Furthermore, in order to fix the casing pipe securely in place within the mold, a wooden stay—either square or round—is used (Fig. 3–A).

A slat of wood with a groove for the cord, and the wooden stay are affixed to the supporting bracket with glue and nails, and then laid across the top of the mold (Fig. 3–B). Another stick the same size as the wooden support is needed in order to flatten out the surface of the concrete before it sets.

Having inserted the casing pipe and placed the supporting bracket in position, the concrete mix should be poured in. Any aggregate used in the concrete should be less than ¾ inch in diameter, and the concrete flattened out with the stick mentioned above.

After being left overnight to dry, the slat with the groove for the cord and the slat supporting the pipe should come away with the supporting bracket. It depends on the type of concrete used, but the mold should be ready for removal after a few days. Fine adjustments can be made with a sander, and the base painted, after it is completely dry (Fig. 4–B).

Construction of the Stem
For this, a piece of bamboo, steel, or aluminum about 1 inch in diameter should be cut to a length of approximately 40 inches, though this will depend both on setting and personal taste. If bamboo is used, the knots must be removed to allow passage of the cord.

When it comes to attaching the socket to the stem of the lamp stand, the type of socket plays an important role. The easiest method is to first decide on the type of socket to be used and then find bamboo or piping that accepts the socket snugly.

If the socket does not fit onto the stem directly, it is best to insert a wooden block in between the socket and the stem, and to attach the socket to this (Fig. 5–B). This may be either square or round, but should have a hole to accommodate the cord. To fix this wooden block to the stem, the kind of metal bracket used to fix towel racks to the wall will work very well (Fig. 5–B1). When fixing the socket in this way, the size of the stem should be determined by the size of the bracket.

Construction of the Shade and Electrical Fixture
For the shade, a sheet of paper about 15–16 inches by 20–25 inches should be rolled up so that the bottom is the width of the stem and the top is much wider (Fig. 6). Since this is such an easy design, one can occasionally change the color and the pattern of the paper. To support this shade, a wire ring may be used. Three holes are drilled through the stem so that the ring is held securely in position (Fig. 7–A). Two of them should be positioned about 6–7 inches below the top of the stem, and the third about 1–2 inches above them. The gap between the bulb and paper shade is determined by the positioning of the two lower holes and the size of the wire ring (Fig. 7–B). Thus it is possible to accommodate different types and strengths of bulbs. The wire ring should be painted the same color as the paper, so as not to clash with the shade.

Having completed all this, all that remains to be done is to thread the cord through the stem and insert a switch between the base and plug. After inserting the socket and bulb, the paper to be used for the shade can be rolled and affixed to the wire ring (Fig. 7–A). The base of the paper shade is attached to the stem with adhesive tape, and the overlap of the rolled paper is glued.

Adaptations
The lamp stand, base and all, may be used in the garden, but, as shown in Fig. 8–A, the cord must emerge from somewhere down the stem when it is inserted directly into the ground. Since there is the danger of the shade being blown about in the wind, one should make liberal use of tape.

It is possible, without changing the design of either the shade or the socket, to attach the stem directly to the wall or to a movable arm attached to the wall. Methods of affixing this arm and the design itself should be evident from studying Fig. 8–B, so we therefore leave readers to experiment for themselves.

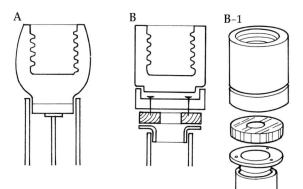

5. (Left) Socket attached directly to stem. (Center and right) If necessary, insert a wooden block between the socket and the stem, and attach the socket to the block. Use a metal bracket to then fix the block to the stem.

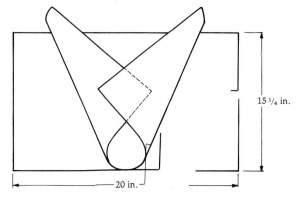

6. Roll up one sheet of paper so that the bottom is the width of the stem, and the top is wider.

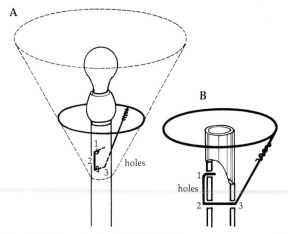

7. Drill three holes (1, 2, 3) in the stem to support the wire ring for the shade. Attach the shade to the ring after threading the cord through the stem, and inserting the socket, bulb, and switch.

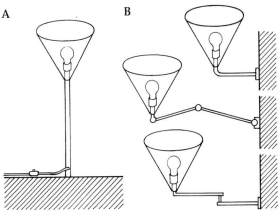

8. (Left) Lampstand inserted into the ground. (Right) Lamps bracketed to the wall.

MATERIALS REQUIRED FOR 12 IN. *CHOCHIN*
   Wood: 1/4 in. × 5 in. × 20 in. (8)
      3/4 in. × 5 in. × 5 in. (2)
   15 or 16 gauge non-electrical
      wire or bamboo: 72 ft.
   Paper
   Glue
TOOLS REQUIRED:
   Saw, jigsaw, cutter

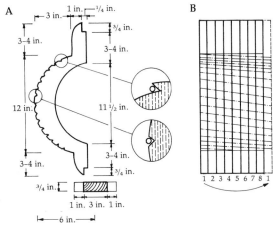

1. (Left) The grooves on each panel must be carefully cut to match the curve of the shade and to ensure that the wire does not slip off. (Right) Marking the panels.

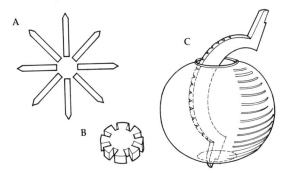

2. The edges of the panels are sharpened, and then the panels are inserted into the stabilizing bases. The diameter of the panels must be less than the diameter of the top opening from which they will be removed.

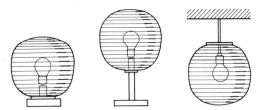

3. *Chochin* may be made into a floor lamp following instructions given in Project 2, or suspended.

PROJECT 4:
Chochin

First, prepare eight panels along the lines of Fig. 1–A, making sure that the width of the panels is less than the diameter of the upper opening of the shade to allow them to be taken out in the end (Fig. 2–C). Grooves must be cut into the panels to hold the bamboo or wire, and the angle of these must accommodate the curve of the shade. In order to wrap the bamboo around the eight panels in a spiral, the grooves must be placed slightly lower on each successive panel (Fig. 1–A). To do this, line up all eight panels as shown in Fig. 1–B. Number the panels and place panel 1 to the right of panel 8. Make horizontal marks at evenly spaced intervals between the two panels. After marking panel 1, return it to its original position. The marks should be on the left side of panel 1 and the right side of panel 8. Draw parallel lines at a slant, connecting each mark on panel 1 with the mark one position lower on panel 8. After sawing lightly along the parallel lines, sharpen the outer edges of the panels (Fig. 2–A). Make the grooves in the indicated positions on the tips of these edges. In addition, a small section should be cut out from the upper and lower inside edges of the panels (Fig. 1–A). These cuts will enable the panels to fit securely into the stabilizing bases.

To make the bases, cut two circular pieces from a board 3/4–1 1/4 inch thick. Measure the circumference of the bases and divide by eight. Mark eight equally spaced intervals on the bases, cut out spaces for the panels (Fig. 2–B), and then insert the panels.

Wrap the bamboo or wire around the panels following the spirally-cut grooves from top to bottom. After forming the first upper circle, secure the loose end with heavy thread. Secure other loose ends in the same way. Attach two loops for affixing the lampshade to an electric bulb to the first circle of the spiral.

For the shade, prepare eight sheets of rectangular paper. Apply slow-drying, white or transparent paste to cover roughly 1/8 of the lampshade. Place the uncut paper on this section, and then cut the paper to size, allowing an overlap of about 1/4 inch between sheets. After the entire lampshade has been papered, and the glue is completely dry, remove the stabilizing bases and then remove the panels through the upper opening. The *chochin* can be suspended from the ceiling, or placed on the floor after a base along the lines of the one described in Project 3 has been added.

4. Frame assembled.

5. Wrapping wire strand.

6. Application of paper.

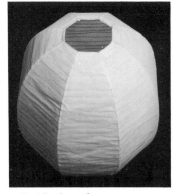

7. Finished product.

BIBLIOGRAPHY

Ashihara, Yoshinobu. *Exterior Design in Architecture*. New York: Van Nostrand Reinhold Co., 1970.

Drexler, Arthur. *The Architecture of Japan*. New York: The Museum of Modern Art, 1954.

Engel, Heinrich. *The Japanese House: A Tradition for Contemporary Architecture*. Tokyo: C. E. Tuttle Co., 1964.

Hashimoto, Fumio. *Architecture in the Shoin Style*. Tokyo and New York: Kodansha International Ltd., 1981.

Hirai, Kiyoshi. *Feudal Architecture of Japan*. Tokyo: Weatherhill/Heibonsha, 1972.

Hughes, Sukey. *Washi: The World of Japanese Paper*. Tokyo and New York: Kodansha International Ltd., 1978.

Itoh, Teiji, and Futagawa, Yukio. *The Essential Japanese House*. Tokyo: John Weatherhill, Inc., 1962.

Itoh, Teiji. *The Elegant Japanese House—Traditional Sukiya Architecture*. New York: Walker/Weatherhill, 1969.

Itoh, Teiji. *Kura: Design and Tradition of the Japanese Storehouse*. Tokyo and New York: Kodansha International Ltd., 1973.

Itoh, Teiji. *Traditional Domestic Architecture of Japan*. Tokyo: Weatherhill/Heibonsha, 1972.

Morse, Edward S. *Japanese Homes and their Surroundings*. Tokyo: C. E. Tuttle Co., 1976.

Naito, Akira. *Katsura, A Princely Retreat*. Tokyo and New York: Kodansha International Ltd., 1977.

Nakashima, George. *The Soul of a Tree: A Woodworker's Reflections*. Tokyo and New York: Kodansha International Ltd., 1981.

Nishihara, Kiyoyuki. *Japanese Houses: Patterns for Living*. Tokyo: Japan Publications Ltd., 1968.

Odate, Toshio. "Japanese Sliding Doors." *Fine Woodworking* 34 (May/June 1982):50–58.

Ota, Hirotaro. *Japanese Architecture and Gardens*. Tokyo: Kokusai Bunka Shinkokai, 1966.

Paine, Robert Treat, and Soper, Alexander. *The Art and Architecture of Japan*. Third Edition. Middlesex, England: Penguin Books, 1981.

Seike, Kiyoshi. *The Art of Japanese Joinery*. Tokyo: Weatherhill/Tankosha, 1977.

Seike, Kiyoshi et al. *A Japanese Touch for Your Garden*. Tokyo and New York: Kodansha International Ltd., 1980.

Suzuki, Daisetsu T. *Zen and Japanese Culture*. Princeton: Princeton University Press, 1973.

Suzuki, Kakichi. *Early Buddhist Architecture*. Tokyo and New York: Kodansha International Ltd., 1980.

Tange, Kenzo, and Kawazoe, Noboru. *Ise: Prototype of Japanese Architecture*. Cambridge, Mass.: The M.I.T. Press, 1965.

Taut, Bruno. *Houses and People of Japan*. Tokyo: Sanseido, 1958.

Yagi, Koji. *Process Architecture, vol. 25 ("Japan: Climate, Space, and Concept")*. Tokyo: Process Architecture Publishing Co., 1981.

Yoshida, Tetsuro. *The Japanese House and Garden*. New York: Praeger, 1969.

From *Boki Ekotoba* (Biography of the Priest Kakunyo), fourteenth century. The priest Kakunyo is shown composing poetry while gazing at some bonsai placed beyond the veranda. Above the veranda are wooden doors which are raised during the day and lowered at night. A brazier with handles has been placed next to Kakunyo.

From *Boki Ekotoba*. As can be seen from this picture, tatami during this period did not yet cover the entire floor. In the middle of the poetry gathering is a brazier. *Sudare* blinds can be seen in the right half of the scroll, and in the upper half, a low table and three hanging scrolls show the beginnings of the *tokonoma*.

FOR FURTHER REFERENCE

For architectural consultation and advice, one may write or call:

The American Institute of Architects
Attn: Member/Component Affairs Dept.
1735 New York Ave., N.W.
Washington, D.C. 20006
(202) 626-7387

For interior decorating assistance, write or call:

NATIONAL HEADQUARTERS:
American Society of Interior Designers
1430 Broadway
New York, NY 10018
(212) 944-9220

CHAPTER PRESIDENTS 1982:

ALABAMA
Robert R. Eckert, ASID
Interior Design Assoc.
120-A North Lafayette St.
(205) 428-3287

ARIZONA NORTH
Melinda Foote, ASID
Foote & Co.
3034 N. Evergreen St.
Phoenix, AZ 85014
(602) 252-6551

ARIZONA SOUTH
Lynda Turrentine, ASID
Interior Concepts
812 N. Crescent Lane
Tucson, AZ 85710
(602) 296-4344

CALIFORNIA-INLAND
Phyllis J. Sullivan, ASID
12330 Sycamore Ave.
Chino, CA 91710
(714) 591-3022

CALIFORNIA-LOS ANGELES
Sherrie Edwards, ASID
Edwards & Assoc.
1100 Alta Loma, 1502
Los Angeles, CA 90069
(714) 846-4285

CALIFORNIA-NORTH
Carl H. Braune, ASID
CAM Designs, Inc.
3645 Grand Ave., Ste. 102
Oakland, CA 94610
(415) 465-6816

CALIFORNIA-ORANGE COUNTY
Daunine Vining, ASID
Daunine Vining & Assoc.
3844 E. Casselle Ave.
Orange, CA 92669
(714) 997-5822

CALIFORNIA-PALM SPRINGS
Herbert Cordier, FASID
2425 Tucsan Rd.
Palm Springs, CA 92262
(714) 933-9914

CALIFORNIA-PASADENA
Constance Ledendecker, ASID
Constance Martin Interiors
4376 Beulah Dr.
La Canada, CA 91011
(213) 790-3258

CALIFORNIA-PENINSULA
Kathleen Malloy, ASID
125 University Ave.
Palo Alto, CA 94301
(415) 321-4131

CALIFORNIA—SAN DIEGO
Marsha Paine, ASID
Nettlecreek
5500 Grossmont Center Dr.
La Mesa, CA 92041
(714) 463-5575

CAROLINAS
Edward H. Springs, ASID
Edward H. Springs Int., Inc.
1236 E. Morehead St.
Charlotte, NC 28204
(704) 376-6461

COLORADO
Elizabeth G. Young, ASID
2317 South Clayton St.
Denver, CO 80210
(303) 623-1200

CONNECTICUT
Theodora L. Graham, ASID
109 Northrop Rd.
Woodbridge, CT 06525
(203) 397-0085

FLORIDA NORTH
Thomas A. Woodruff, ASID
947 Greenridge Rd.
Jacksonville, FL 32207
(904) 396-3051

FLORIDA SOUTH
William F. Andrews, ASID
100 N.E. Fifth Ave.
Delray Beach, FL 33444
(305) 276-5823

GEORGIA
Charles D. Gandy, ASID
C. Gandy & Assoc.
1411 Dutch Valley Pl., N.E.
Atlanta, GA 30324
(404) 874-1946

HAWAII
Emmett R. Herrera, ASID
Architects Hawaii, Ltd.
190 S. King St., Ste. 300
Honolulu, HI 96813
(808) 523-9636

ILLINOIS
John T. Caruso, ASID
625 E. Central Ave.
Lombard, IL 60148
(312) 644-1526

INDIANA
Janie Jacobs, ASID
Bob Arehart Assoc., Inc.
902 East 66th St.
Indianapolis, IN 46220
(317) 257-1186

LOUISIANA
Judy Girod, ASID
Judy Girod Interior Des., Inc.
1070 St. Charles Ave., Ste. F
New Orleans, LA 70130
(504) 524-8642

MARYLAND
Sondra M. Shochet, ASID
Village of Cross Keys
1 Village Square, Ste. 109
Baltimore, MD 21210
(301) 433-0063

MICHIGAN
Brian Clay Collins, ASID
222 West St.
Northville, MI 48167
(313) 425-4242

MINNESOTA
Gary E. Wheeler, ASID
Wheeler-Hildebrandt Design
10 South 5th St., 854
Minneapolis, MN 55402
(612) 373-2030

MISSOURI EAST
Lloyd F. Barling, ASID
Barling Assoc., Inc.
211 Old Meramec Station Rd.
Manchester, MO 63011
(314) 227-5711

MISSOURI WEST/KANSAS
Jack Madison Rees, ASID
Jack Rees Interiors
4501 Belleview
Kansas City, MO 64111
(816) 651-3035

NEBRASKA/IOWA
Thomas D. Klemuk, ASID
305 Main St.
Cedar Falls, IA 50613
(319) 266-7573

NEW ENGLAND
William P. Grimes, ASID
Design Assoc., Inc.
281 Belmont St.
Belmont, MA 02178
(617) 484-3234

NEW JERSEY
Charles Van Buskirk, ASID
2 Audubon Pl.
Fair Lawn, NJ 07410
(201) 797-3612

NEW MEXICO
Craig F. Zupan, ASID
4821 Crest S.E. #5
Albuquerque, NM 87108
(505) 242-7522

NEW YORK METROPOLITAN
David Eugene Bell, ASID
Design Multiples, Inc.
345 East 69th St.
New York, NY 10021
(212) 288-8690

NY UPSTATE/CANADA EAST
Fred B. Hershey, ASID
Burlington Interiors, Inc.
302 State St.
Albany, NY 12210
(518) 436-1448

OHIO NORTH
Charles B. Whitmore, ASID
1228 Quilliams Rd.
Cleveland, OH 44121
(216) 382-6600

OHIO SOUTH/KENTUCKY
Gayle S. Kreutzfeld, ASID
2595 Dorset Rd.
Columbus, OH 43221
(614) 258-8210

OKLAHOMA
Sally G. Taggart, ASID
Sally Taggart Int. Des.
3305 South Peoria
Tulsa, OK 74105
(918) 747-6550

OREGON
Russell L. Emmert, ASID
2920 S.W. Dolph Ct.
Portland, OR 97219
(503) 245-7602

PENNSYLVANIA EAST
Bertram Laudenslager, ASID
Whitemarsh Interiors, Inc.
1521 Bethlehem Pike
Flourtown, PA 19031
(215) 247-5415

PENNSYLVANIA WEST
Nancy Hoff Barsotti, ASID
32 Edgecliff Rd.
Carnegie, PA 15106
(412) 881-0100

POTOMAC
Odette Lueck, ASID
Odette Lueck Interiors
13305 Old Chapel Rd.
Bowie, MD 20715
(301) 262-5280

TENNESSEE
David A. Stearns, ASID
McCormick-Eubanks
1793 Union Ave.
Memphis, TN 38104
(901) 274-6518

TEXAS
Arlis Ede, FASID
Arlis Ede Interiors
3520 Fairmount
Dallas, TX 75219
(214) 521-1302

TEXAS GULF COAST
Jana See Willibey, ASID
Mary Ann Bryan, Interiors
4041 Richmond Ave.
Houston, TX 77027
(713) 622-8184

UTAH
Bruce Edwards, ASID
B. J. Edwards Environments
1419 Yale Ave.
Salt Lake City, UT 84105
(801) 583-3592

VIRGINIA
G. Reese Fowler, ASID
GRF Designs
5104 S. Lake Rd.
Virginia Beach, VA 23455
(804) 464-3463

WASHINGTON STATE
Barbara A. Sauerbrey, FASID
1527 121st St.
Bellevue, WA 98005
(206) 747-0324

WISCONSIN
Harriet R. Weiss, ASID
8007 N. Port Washington Rd.
Milwaukee, WI 53217
(414) 351-0227

INDEX

(plate numbers are in bold type)